Rogues,
Rascals&
Rare
Gems

Rogues, Rascals& Rare Gems

Danny Unrau

Everyday People Looking For An Everyday God

KINDRED
PRODUCTIONS

WINNIPEG, MANITOBA   HILLSBORO KANSAS

Kindred Productions is the publishing arm for the Mennonite Brethren Churches. Kindred publishes, promotes and markets print and mixed media resources that help shape our Christian faith and discipleship from the Mennonite Brethren perspective.

Rogues, Rascals & Rare Gems
Copyright © 1999 by Kindred Productions, Winnipeg, Manitoba, Canada

Published simultaneously by Kindred Productions, Winnipeg, Manitoba R2L 2E5 and Kindred Productions, Hillsboro, KS 67063.

Book and cover design by Fred Koop, Winnipeg, MB.
Printed by Hignell Printing Limited, Winnipeg, MB.

Canadian Cataloguing in Publication Data

Unrau, Danny, 1950 -

Rogues, rascals & rare gems: everyday people looking for an everyday God

ISBN 0-921788-57-6

1. Christian life - Anecdotes. I. Title. II: Rogues, rascals and rare gems

BV4517.U57 1999   242   C99-920035-6

International Standard Book Number: 0-921788-57-6

Contents

Introduction

On any ordinary day one can meet an extraordinary person, whether that person be exceptionally kind, angry, courageous, compassionate, mysterious, tactless, hungry, hopeful or passionate. People, all of whom are made in the image of God, are by definition extraordinary and their beings, their stories when encountered prove again that truth is better than fiction. The people in this little book, whom I affectionately and interchangeably call rogues, rascals and rare gems, have all added to my life. These true stories have become part of my story; these rich personalities have informed my personality. They have all gifted me with some richness I did not have before I met them, whether I was still a child, a kind of youthful adventurer traveling in faraway countries, or a teacher and clergyman trying to read life for its stories and lessons about the creation and the Creator.

It warms me to think that everyone, no matter where they live, no matter how they live, regardless of the personality and the experiences they have been given, are looking for meaning and purpose. And that search somehow leads us back to the Source from which we came so that life can make sense. Some of us are searching wisely, some of us foolishly—though none of us doing both all the time. We humans are all everyday people and I see us looking for a God for every day. To find God is to find that life makes sense. That sense making then orders everything else we do.

I hope you enjoy these ordinary rogues, rascals and rare gems as much as I did and still do. Let their stories inform your story and consider, if you will, how it is that God is calling us all back to himself. Please know that sometimes I have changed names to protect the identity of the innocent. Please also note that I refer to God using the traditional masculine pronoun. I would like to remind you, however, that God should not be restricted to the limitations of human sexuality. God is more than being male or female. He has made all men and women, boys and girls; he has poured himself, and still does, into all these people making the world richer with the existence of everyone, every day.

Wild Al

Al is fifty, by no means looking older than his age, though he is balding and a little gaunt, his slenderness partially left over from a serious illness a few years ago. But he walks tall and shows his six feet-something well. He could easily pass as being athletic.

Al was upstairs in his bedroom changing into clothes appropriate for some dirty work, finding some grubby trousers and an old T-shirt in his closet, when he heard the yelp of a security house alarm outside. He glanced out the front window of his upstairs bedroom and noted the white van backed up the driveway of the neighbor's house across the street. He thought nothing of it.

When the alarm started up a second time, he looked out again, and this time it dawned on him that the white van was not the vehicle his neighbors owned. Pulling on a shirt, Al moved down the stairs to look out the small glass window of his front door, to get a better look at the van and see what was going on, the awareness growing in him that a break-and-enter might be occurring. The van's front license plate was bent down so he could not read the blue numbers and letters on the white background. He opened his front door and walked straight out, across his lawn, over the street and toward the white vehicle.

By this time, a couple of young men had come scurrying out of the house, arms loaded with computer components. Al noticed the front door and its entire frame had been bashed out of the entranceway of the house. He hurried forward to get the van's license number; registering instinctively that such information would now be crucial in the aftermath of the crime being committed.

As Al approached the van and was bending over in his half run to read the license number, the vehicle lurched forward. The driver had seen him coming just as the two thieving partners jumped into the van and started to make his getaway. But Al was on the driveway; there was no way he could get out of the way, the van was already moving too quickly and Al was too close to escape. With a pilot's quick reaction, Al leapt onto the front bumper as the driver gunned the truck toward him. The forward motion of the van and Al's motion of stepping up propelled him, arms and legs flailing, up the slanted front of the van, over the windshield and onto the top of the vehicle. Luckily the rails of the car top carrier on the mini-van were easily grasped as Al prevented himself from sliding right along the length of the vehicle and off the back. The driver slammed on the brakes, hoping to dislodge this wild man suddenly on the roof of his getaway van, and certainly not a person factored into the planning of this crime. By this time, Al was clinging to the van roof rails with adrenaline force and kicking huge dents into the roof with his feet. The driver realized the spider-man on his roof would not be easily dislodged and turned onto 49th Ave., weaving the vehicle back and forth, alternately slamming on the brakes and accelerating, hoping to clear his roof of his human cargo and make a clean getaway at the same time. People walking the quiet sidewalks of this upper-end neighborhood were struck by the sounds of squealing tires and slamming brakes, over the screams of a man, all arms and legs on top of a careening van.

"Call the police! Call the police!" screamed Al over the profanity of one of the vehicle's occupants hanging out the passenger side window shouting, "Old man, get the _ off our van!"

Finally realizing he couldn't shake his passenger parasite, the robber driver pulled into a quieter street, slammed on the brakes and stopped. Jumping out, the three hooligans surrounded the van on three sides. Al was now standing twelve feet tall on the van roof looking down at the snarling thieves waiting to pounce when he would come down. The name-calling, the cursing continued. Al danced about on the roof of the vehicle, not at all sure he wanted to come down. Savior cars would surely be coming down this street eventually.

He targeted the widest opening in a gap between his triangle of attackers and jumped from the roof of the vehicle like a stunt man. But his ankle buckled. Al fell. But he had started to scramble to his feet even before he hit the ground. The three amigos came at him. In getting up, his sleeve pulled up and Al's watch came into full view of the closest mugger bearing down on him. Always on the lookout for high-priced products to pick for free, the would-be assailant recognized Al's watch as a diamond studded Rolex. The mugger froze, his killer instinct outflanked by the beauty of the booty now suddenly available for the picking. "Get the Rolex! Get the Rolex!" he added to his string of screaming expletives and urban war cries. The change in goal paralyzed his partner muggers for the half-second Al needed to gain his feet and start running. By this time cars were pulling up next to the debacle and the three thieves suspended their assault, jumped back into their van and sped away.

Al leaned against a tree, panting. The first passer-by, cell phone in hand, jumped out of his car and put his hand on Al's shoulder.

"I saw that! Are you okay?"

"I can stand the cursing," Al panted. "I can even understand that they wanted to kill me for messing with their fun. But they called me Old Man! Ooh, that really gets me! That re-eally gets me. Did you get their license number?"

One of the problems of living in affluence is that we have stuff people can take away from us and when people take our stuff away, we get upset. The upsetness is caused not only because our possessions are convenient to us for practical reasons, but because we have come to use them as ways of defining ourselves. Possessions are often our signboards and symbols of how we want our watching world to see us and know something about us in socio-economic terms without us having to explain ourselves. What this also means is that we watch out for others, especially those who are in our own circles. We enter into a social contract to help protect our neighbors' property and when a neighbor is getting his possessions pilfered, we try to stop the violation. We do this not only for material reasons, but because we value neighborliness.

That is what Al did that day, although without a careful enough sense of his own safety. Al was only trying to be a good neighbor, but he became a poor steward of his own life. Al was grieving the mindset that one can take what one can grab even if it belongs to someone else. Al was standing up against a perspective that thinks there is no immorality in violating others' property and person. Al was protesting against rape of every kind and he is lucky to be alive.

Al is a purist; he wants things to be the way they are set to be. He wants people to live politely and properly. He might even want a God who stands over the world and keeps the pieces moving the way they should be moved; a God who will not just stand by and let the pieces fall off the table or get thrown around the room.

When Al ran across the road to catch the thieves and when his attackers insulted him, he was calling out to God to make the world a better place, a more perfect place. A place where we humans are no longer vandals, but stewards and good neighbors. That's what God will do someday. He promises he will make it all right. In that sense, then, he is the God for today and everyday, because someday it will be made right. The unrightnesses of today will be corrected tomorrow. And we won't need any of our things then either.

Kurt

"One of our old family friends has a son living here in Vancouver. The son, whose name is Kurt, has cancer and has had one of his legs amputated. Could you talk to any of these people if they called you? Could I give them your name and number?" came the question.

The call didn't come for six months or so, but it came. Late one evening.

"Dad! Someone on the phone for you. I don't know who it is."

"Hello!"

"My name is Elva. I don't know if you remember Albert talking about us, but I'm the mom whose son has cancer. I don't really know why I'm calling, but I'd like to meet with you. Would that be possible? I'd prefer to meet you here at the hospital. Kurt is here, and so is his girlfriend, Angela."

An hour later we were sitting together in the waiting room of the palliative care ward of a large hospital. Meetings like this are always awkward. We didn't know each other, this mourning and tormented mother and I, and the subject at hand wasn't made for small talk. A son was dying; a girlfriend was frightened; a mom seemed to be feeling too many things too strongly to identify them all.

"As a clergyman, I can do a number of things for you if you like," I told Elva. "I can talk with any, or all of you, about life and death, mostly death, at this point, if you wish, or I can just be around and be quiet if you like. I will offer you whatever you think someone in my position should do. But I will not push myself or my views upon you. You'll have to let me know what you want."

"I think you should meet Kurt and Angela," Elva said. "I think they would like to get married before he goes. About talking, I'm not sure anybody wants to talk about the other thing. Come, meet Kurt."

I walked into the hospital room. A tall man, young, in his late twenties or early thirties, with dark thick hair and a reddish beard, lay on the bed one leg pulled up towards his chest, the other ending in a stump just above where the knee used to be. He raised his head, smiled weakly and wondered, I think, through his morphined perceptions, who I was and what I wanted. Angela, careful, quiet and gently shy, hovered around, wondering about the rules of relationship in this kind of a meeting. I offered my help to the two of them and took my leave when it seemed appropriate.

A few days later Elva was on the phone again.

"Could you perform a wedding ceremony for Kurt and Angela? He's at home now. He won't go back to the hospital. There's not a lot of time left, but they'd really like to get married. Would Saturday at one o'clock work for you?"

Early Saturday afternoon I pulled out of the suburbs and headed into the east end of the city, described by some as the most impoverished postal code

zone in Canada. I found a parking place a block or so
away from the address I was given on Mercantile
Drive.

Stepping over discarded toys and clothes, walking
past street sellers of sex and old shoes and ethnic
restaurants and coffeeshops blaring their music and
exuding their various notable smells into the street, I
found the low doorway leading to Kurt's apartment.
The doorway opened into a courtyard crisscrossed
with stairways and clotheslines. The courtyard had
been painted bright turquoise many years ago; now
containers with geraniums added some natural color
to the scene. I found the door with the number I had
been given and knocked. A tinny reverberation from
the metal door echoed around the courtyard and
mixed with the sounds of the street.

The door opened and I ducked into a smallish
apartment. A hallway crammed with the stuff of day-
to-day living led straight into the living room. "Living
room," I thought, "I have never thought of that label
before in relationship to 'dying room,' which it is today. Dying room, not living room." Stale cigarette
smoke permeated the room. Its smell was so thick it
felt like something that slows you down when you
walk, or what it must feel like if someone put a lead
weight in your lungs to make breathing harder. A leg
prosthesis with a flexible knee and a proud new soccer
shoe on its foot stood in a corner, looking like it was
ready to run. Purring around the room, tails held
high, ends twitching back and forth, two black cats
owned and paced the place around and over Kurt lying on a mat on the floor. He looked no stronger than
he had in the hospital. Angela sat on the couch over-
looking Kurt and his mat. I was introduced to the
new faces in the room I had not met before.

"Well, Angela, are we here for a wedding?" I asked

after the niceties were exchanged.

"Yes!" she smiled.

"Legally, all we need to do is sign the papers, if you have them, and it's done, or would you like to exchange vows and have a few words spoken?"

"I think some vows should be said," answered Angela, putting a smile at the end of her sentence.

I filled out the marriage registration forms and made small talk with the people around me, asking addresses, writing out parents' birthplaces and mothers' maiden names for a fastidious Department of Vital Statistics. Kurt remained still and unmoving on his mat. I got down on the floor close to him, greeted him and asked him about getting married. He smiled weakly. I began the ritual, long familiar for someone in my profession but today taking on new meaning.

"Do you, Kurt, take Angela to be your wife, to love and receive from, until death do you part?" Kurt nodded. The phrase "till death do you part" frogged up my throat; it had never seemed so profound, so real before. Most couples getting married find it easy to answer that one. They don't really believe that they will die, or at least, not for a long, long time.

"Do you, Angela, take Kurt to be your husband, to nurture and nurse and care for and sustain, until death do you part?"

"I do!" she smiled, eyes full of tears. Tears of happiness; tears of sadness. I suspected that as a little girl this wasn't the way she had imagined her wedding day. This was more; this was less.

"Do you have rings?" I asked. Angela fumbled for a box hidden in the folds of the blankets on the couch and produced two rings. Fighting back tears, she gently picked up Kurt's weak left arm and tenderly placed the ring on his passive finger. She pushed the ring that seemed oversized now over the first and then the sec-

ond finger joint. Then she put her ring just on the
end of her wedding band finger. Reaching around
with her other hand, she cupped Kurt's right hand in
hers and guided his fingers over her ring and pushed
it into place on her hand. Now the tears were flowing
freely. Kurt was roused and stimulated by the action
and he looked intensely at his ring. He began to
stroke it with weak fingers from his right hand, seem-
ingly buoyed by the energy of the event, buoyed by the
deep consciousness that Angela was true in her devo-
tion to care for him, to love him.

"Well, let's sign these papers," I interjected as Angela leaned back onto the couch beside the mat on
which the groom lay, who now was just looking
blankly at the wall, but carefully and affectionately still
touching his ring.

Angela signed her place on the Marriage Registration. I moved down onto Kurt's mat. Lying half beside him and half behind him, I reached one arm under and around him to take his right hand in mine,
and with my other hand I pushed a pen into his
curled fingers. He tried to prop himself up on one
shaky elbow. Holding the Marriage Registration with
my left hand, I steadied Kurt's hand as he signed his
name, probably for the last time. As Kurt settled back
down onto his mat, I moved to a sister and a mom to
witness the event. They all cried; we all cried. Joy over
love and commitment and promise mingled with sadness at the stark dead-endedness of this marriage.

"By the powers vested in me by the Government of
British Columbia and by the responsibilities charged
me by God, I pronounce you, Kurt and Angela, husband and wife. May your days together be days of caring, compassion, tenderness and love."

With the tones of a seasoned but sometimes reluc-
tant religious leader, I spoke a prayer, a benediction

17

over the new couple, inviting God to lay his gentle hand on these two lovers for the time they still had together. We, the two witnesses and the small group of family members and friends, visited for a few minutes. Angela smiled through her tears, while others sniffed through their nervous, wanting-to-be-and-even-being-a-little-happy-in-spite-of-everything laughter. Kurt lay on his mat, unmoving, his right hand holding his left, his married hand, cradling his ring. His eyes were still fixed on the wall.

It was in the brief afterglow of the little wedding that I noticed for the first time that the wall behind me, the wall one would have to turn away from Kurt to see, contained a display case—of human skulls. Dozens of plastic, plaster and papier-mâché replicas of the human skull, ranging in size from that of a large egg to that of an actual adult human, made up the macabre display. Some expression of a sense of humor was intended from the collection it seemed, but in the context of the skull's dark symbolism well-known to some segments of North American subculture and in the context of real impending death, it made the living room a shocking kind of Golgotha. Did Kurt somehow know long ago that this room would be the room of his death?

I said, "Goodbye!" after staying some time and walked out into the Saturday sunshine of Mercantile Drive.

The telephone will one day have to confess to being technology's greatest news bearer, for a few days later mine rang again.

"Angela would like you to baptize Kurt. Do you think you could do that? He's really not doing that well." I assured my caller I would be there shortly. Before leaving the house, however, I prepared a small container with olive oil for anointing and began to protectively prepare myself for the kind of emotions and profound life pictures one sees around the coming of death.

The day was already late when I turned onto Mercantile Drive. The sidewalks were busy with the not so uncommon business of the night so often found in areas of urban decay like this one. Clearly the people here lived in urban poverty, yet a certain defiance paraded itself brazenly along these sidewalks and in front of these pawnshops, tawdry secondhand stores and colorful ethnic eating places. All the symbols of socioeconomic hardship were present under every street light and perched at every alley entrance. People of all ages worked the street looking for the rewards but paying dearly the costs of their particular trades around the smells and the sounds of depravation and poverty, pain and hopelessness.

There was room to park on the street close to Kurt's dwelling this time and I stepped over discarded instruments of the life on the street and ducked through the doorway into the now familiar turquoise courtyard. This time I knew where the door was.

Familiar faces and a few new ones greeted me inside the now familiar dwelling place. I shook hands around the room, moved past the skulls on my left, and turned towards Kurt on my right, still lying on the mat where I had performed his nuptials. He was awake. And alert. His large eyes, exaggerated by his shrunken cheeks and pronounced cheekbones, were animated and active.

I bent close to him and touched his shoulder.

"Hello, Kurt," I said, "remember me?"

"Yeah," he said in more of a groan than a statement, "Yeah, and I have a wife, a wife!" He was remembering my face in connection to the marriage of a few days ago as he fought the morphine in his system,

19

trying to clear his memory, his awareness.

"Angela wants me to baptize you, Kurt, and I'd like to talk to you about God. Do you want to talk about God?" He looked at me with unreadable eyes. I spoke slowly. "I've been told that you've been angry at God about your cancer, about the treatments, about the pain, and I don't know about other things as well, but everything is a little different now." I stopped. His eyes watched mine. "You don't have much time left." Testing whether he was facing his reality squarely, I went on. "Would you like to say, 'Whatever, God, I give up. It's up to you, whoever you are, to do what you want with my life now. I can't fight this; I can't do this anymore. So I'm yours.' Would you like to consider God, and say, 'Yes' to God, and make peace with everything and let it all end peacefully?" I hesitated again, watching his eyes for some sign that these words were touching him, whether this was a welcome conversation, or whether he felt violated by it. I couldn't read his eyes. "Would you like to think about all this? Would you like some time to think about what God might have to do with you in all this?" I perceived a nod. He needed some time.

A sister of Kurt's lay down on the mat beside him.

"Say yes! to God, Kurt. It'll be good for you; it'll be good for Angela. Just say, Yes! to God." Kurt's brow furrowed and the look of deep thought now showed clearly on his face. He settled his cheek against his pillow, but the look of intense searching stayed. I moved onto the couch beside his mat and waited. The family and friends looked to me to do something, to keep moving. I just waited. Moments crawled on. Kurt's thoughtful eyes stared at the wall.

Suddenly, Kurt started grasping at his sister's hand.

"Do you want to say yes! to God, Kurt?" she asked. Kurt nodded. His sister beckoned me to the floor beside him, her gesturing almost desperate.

"I don't know if you know the story of Jesus nailed to the cross, Kurt," I said. "But when Jesus was being executed, nails through his feet and hands holding him onto a wooden cross, his pain a lot like yours, they also hung two thieves, each on a cross on either side of him in a multiple public execution. The two thieves saw Jesus suffer. There seemed to be some kind of bond between these three men dying together in public, and they communicated with one another. The one thief, angry and bitter, it seems, was annoyed and severely irritated by this Jesus and he defied him, cursed him, but the other one, also a convicted thief, obviously getting what he deserved for the sake of justice, cried out, 'Remember me, Jesus, when you get to where you're going! When you get to your Kingdom.' And Jesus answered, 'Today you will go with me wherever I go! Today you will get into paradise with me!' Is that what you think you'd like? To go into a perfect place with God, Kurt?"

He nodded his head ever so slightly. His eyes blinked a "yes!"

"Well, that's it, then, Kurt. You have said Yes! to God. God doesn't gather round himself people who are good, he gathers round himself people who just say, 'Help!'"

"Could someone hand me that glass of water?" I asked, pointing to the glass on the coffee table, beside a wicker basket of innumerable pharmaceutical products. The oversized blue plastic drinking glass was handed to me and I dipped my fingers into its water. "Upon your nod to God, then, I baptize you, Kurt, in the name of the Father, the Son, and the Holy Spirit."

I dribbled the water on his forehead with my right hand and dabbed the water running down onto his pillow with a paper towel with the other hand. Kurt trembled as the water touched his hot forehead. Then he settled down into his blanket, his head relaxing deeply into the pillow.

"Our Father," I began, "who art in heaven..." Voices around the room joined in. With the gallery of skulls looking on, we prayed together the Jesus prayer permitting God's will, invoking the mysterious power and explicable glory of God into the room that until this minute was owned by death, but now, I sensed, was being replaced with warm eternal light and some good hope. With the "Amen!" the room became quiet.

Outside the window we could hear the business people of the night street negotiating their deals. Angela sat with her eyes closed. Tears coursed down her cheeks, her lips moved in a practiced prayer. Her shoulders pulled up, her body language was tearfully celebratory and tormented. Now I reached into my pocket for the small container of olive oil, a homemade chrism, popped off the lid and said, "Kurt, I'm going to anoint you with oil for your new journey with God, for your journey to heaven that you have just started on." Sticking a thumb into the container I signed the cross on Kurt's forehead with the oil and stepped back.

Kurt never moved. The assembly became quiet and thoughtful again. A kind of serenity entered the room. No one spoke. We sat in silence. Kurt lay still and quiet on his mat, staring as if into a far distance. I sat on the couch thinking thoughts of other deaths, other times of trouble, other times of encountering God.

Beside me on the end of the couch lay a modern and partial version of the Bible entitled *The Message of Hope* (Colorado Springs: NavPress, 1994). I picked it up and flipped through its pages. I started to read aloud. The words tolled out their gentle peace, "God,

investigate my life...I'm an open book to you; even
from a distance, you know what I'm thinking...If I
climb to the sky, you're there! If I go underground,
you're there! If I flew on morning's wings to the far
western horizon, You'd find me in a minute—you're already there waiting...See for yourself whether I've
done anything wrong—then guide me on the road to
eternal life...God, my shepherd! I don't need a
thing...Even when the way goes through Death Valley,
I'm not afraid when you walk at my side...Your beauty
and love chase after me every day of my life. I'm back
home in the house of God for the rest of my life...But
the truth is that Christ has been raised up, the first in
a long legacy of those who are going from death to
life...." I stopped reading. Nobody spoke. We drank
in the peace of the silence. Kurt lay still on the floor,
unperturbed.

"Do you have the poem *Footsteps* in that book?"
somebody asked, almost in a whisper. I shook my
head. Angela jumped up and left the room. The rest
of us waited in the silence, unmoving. Angela came
back carrying the requested poem, mounted within a
frame that stands on a shelf or a dresser.

"Kurt bought this for me," she smiled, tears running down her face. She handed it to me. I read the
poem. When the words "that's when I carried you..."
echoed around the room, sobs and sniffles added
their voices to the quiet. We sat on. Kurt breathed
deeply and regularly. We wondered how long it would
take. Minutes became an hour. I excused myself and
left.

Out on the street, a man ran by me with a fist full
of money. A small child, hours past what should have
been his bedtime, sat with his feet in the gutter. A
newspaper had blown up against the front tire of my
car. Two young lovers, oblivious to the world, saun-

23

tered by, leaning into each other, talking intensely and enjoying each other's company.

I started the car and moved slowly in the direction of my suburban world where even marriages and deaths seem cleaner.

Kurt rallied the next day, I was told later. He got up and moved around the apartment. He seemed revived, renewed. Then he worsened. Three days later the telephone rang again. "Can you conduct the funeral for us?"

We gathered at a funeral home and took over the chapel. The family wanted some of his music played, his sister had written a eulogy. The coffin was open. Someone predicted that only 25 or so people would come. In the end there were more than a hundred. Metal rock aficionados mainly, tattooed, wearing black T-shirts sporting the logo of the band Kurt played in, black leather jackets, hats, mostly baseball hats on backwards, and rings, earrings and noserings, nearly filled the chapel. It was easy to see that no one was in familiar or comfortable surroundings, but on the other hand a resolute determination to master the situation hung in the room. Obviously a bond and an affection for Kurt or Angela or their respective families drew them to this place, and there seemed no risk that they wouldn't stay throughout the ritual that was about to be played out.

After some moments of rather soft recorded rock music, the funeral director nodded that I should begin the proceedings. I squeezed past the coffin, open with symbols of Kurt's life and loves around him: guitar picks in a pattern on his chest, a picture of Angela in his hand and his own recently recorded cassette tape beside him among other mementos and metaphors of his life and affections.

I cleared my throat, straightened my little book of

notes on the podium and studied the typed obituary-tribute that Kurt's sister had handed me.

"I'm the religious guy here," I started, "and I'm guessing that none of us in this room wants to be here. We'd rather be anywhere else. But because Kurt died, we're here, and because he died, there is no better place to be right now. We are here to say goodbye to Kurt; we're here because it is permissible to cry about, to get angry about, his death, his cancer, his suffering, our loss. It's probably true that all of you in this room knew Kurt better than I did, but I passed through some profound rites of passage with Kurt in the last ten days or so, and because they're not the kinds of things that you went through with him, I feel that I, too, have walked some significant steps with our friend, Kurt." I talked about Kurt's wedding, and his baptism, his "nodding toward God," all on his apartment floor, making a reference to the irony of a priest-like kind of guy working within the sight and even the reach of all those skulls. At the mention of the skulls and the irony of my work, many in the crowd smiled. Some cried.

"I'll talk a little here today. Then I'll invite any of you to 'remember Kurt' if you want. Then I'll read some of the Bible poetry that was read in his room in those past few days, I'll pray a prayer for Kurt and for us, and then we'll go to the cemetery for the burial."

After my few reflections, I read Kurt's sister's account of her brother's life, before his dad took the podium and between his prepared and kind words profoundly and deeply mourned the loss of his son, expressing the grief that flows so naturally out of deep loss and sadness. His words and his anguish articulated much of what most of the young people in the room were feeling, and were a part of in their own private expression. Then friends took turns pouring out their heartfelt love for Kurt, remembering his gifts, his spirit, his character, his friendship. A band member, ending his tribute, held up his right hand with middle fingers curled down and the index and little finger raised, announced, "Metal Rules!"

Another family friend pointed out, "Though Kurt was known to all of you as bright and gifted, you should know that Kurt was also wise. Wise in the way he brought complete and good closure to his relationship with Angela, with God and with life. Kurt was wise!"

Young men with all the trappings of a tough society were unafraid to cry. They were courageous enough to express their grief. Everyone politely listened to or even joined in the Scriptures read and prayers spoken. The chapel felt warm in its loving remembrance of Kurt.

After Ozzy Osborne's rendition of "See You On the Other Side" was wept through, the funeral director instructed the assembled mourners that the service would end by each one moving out through the front of the chapel to pay their last respects to Kurt and speak their condolences to Angela and the family. The Black Jackets all moved forward in respectful procession. Many of them touched Kurt in his coffin; nearly all wept openly with Angela and the family members.

One of the pallbearers stepped up to where I stood at the side of the chapel a few feet away from the coffin and muttered something to the effect, "Good words!" before returning to his seat. Then suddenly he was beside me again, "We've really got to start drinking!" I smiled. I had said enough.

As the mourners wound their way out of the chapel, Kurt's band members handed out copies of their cassette tape for people to play in their cars as they drove to the cemetery. At the cemetery, we huddled around the gravesite, said and heard a few more words, prayed one more prayer, and stood aside as all of Kurt's friends, instructed again by the funeral director, filed past the coffin and scattered small handfuls of sand on the cover of their friend's shiny, wooden final bed. Then we just stood in silence.

From across the peaceful green funeral gardens and from the open door of a car parked on the nearest driveway, wafted the sound of heavy metal music "for Kurt!" We continued to stand in silence, all of us, for some time. Then knots of smaller and larger groups started to drift away to their cars and back to their lives. Kurt's life was put away, but not his memory, nor his journey.

W e are a death-denying culture and we are always surprised when death, which we are powerless against, comes knocking. The only choice we have is to accept it or not accept it. Even so, our attitude changes nothing in death's march. Death takes its own journey with everyone; we will all travel the route at some time or another.

While a determination to live is helpful in staving off a too-soon death, at some point that determination becomes counterproductive to acceptance and peace. To accept death, to be at peace with it, even when it is too early or too painful, comes from wisdom. Wisdom, as the songwriter says, is knowing when to hold, when to close and when to fold. Timing is nearly everything. But wisdom is more than that. Wisdom is tying all the loose ends: with ourselves, with our families, with our friends, with our neighbors, with our God. When unfinished matters are finished, death

27

can be entered into and accepted like a peaceful friend, and tragedy is chased from the room.

I think that is what Kurt did and I think he died a peaceful death; he knew his life was complete. That doesn't mean he couldn't have done more and it doesn't mean that Angela and his mother and father and his friends don't miss him terribly and cry out in their personal loneliness for him, but, in a hard situation it ended as good as it could have.

"Accept, forgive and love" are a triangle of watchwords to make our lives work well. If these three swirl brightly in the colors of our life, we can smile and sigh when it must end. When Jesus walked a hard, dry and dusty land that wouldn't accept him, that couldn't forgive him, that wouldn't love him, he died, but his rising gave acceptance, forgiveness and love to the whole human world forever, free for the asking. Life is hard for most of us, if not all of us, at some time or another, but to live it everyday with Jesus, and to grasp and touch and hold what he gives, makes living a song instead of a dirge, and a dance instead of a march.

The Royal Banker

My kids wanted me to get their bankbooks updated, they wanted to know how much their respective accounts of $17.34, $29.59 and $78.46 had accumulated in interest since the last time we checked, and I needed $50 in cash, so I went to the bank on No. 3 Road.

Now the bank on No. 3 Road in Richmond, B.C. has three ATMs (automated teller machines) and one automated bankbook updater, so I knew I could get all my banking done in one stop. My intention, upon entering the bank, was to update the little blue and gold books first, but the updater was occupied. Not wanting to waste any time, I shifted my plans and moved to get the cash I wanted from the ATM nearest the Updater. Just as I was finishing my transaction, the Updater came free so I quickly stepped over to it and started to read the directions. I was not as familiar with this machine as I was with the ATM. Just as I was guiding the first little blue book into the slot on the Updater for printing, the ATM closest to me started screaming. Screaming as if it were a desperate fire truck or a panicky ambulance. Stepping back from the Updater and looking curiously at the noisemaker, I noticed that the lips of the nearest ATM were holding a small stack of bills. I stepped closer to investigate. Isn't it every person's dream to walk up to an ATM and see money already waiting to be removed from this magical machine that seems to give on command? I reached for the money, flipped the edges of the bills, noting there were two twenties and two five-dollar bills. Looking around the small bank foyer and waiting room and seeing no one there who could have just been standing at the machine, I looked out through the plate glass wall into the parking lot. Just getting into their car were the two women who had been at the Updater just before me. Maybe it was their money, I thought. I ran out through the swinging bank doors and out to the women in the parking lot. I tapped on the driver's window of the car starting to back out of its parking spot. "Is this your money, that you left in the bank machine?"

The driver shook her head, "No!"

I returned to the bank feeling somewhat defeated. Those who had been standing in line behind me were now watching me with some curiosity, I thought. Bemused curiosity, I think now.

"Hmm," I said to them as I came back into the bank, "Whoever's money this is, must be already gone."

Two Brinks guards just coming into the bank noted with some interest this man holding fifty dollars in the air, talking to the five or so people in the bank.

"What's the problem?" one of the Brink's guards asked.

"Someone seems to have left their money in the ATM and left without it," I volunteered, as something warm and silly started to dawn on me. "Oh, my goodness," I said, "it's my money. I left it in there!"

"Sure you did!" said the Brink's guard, his tone indicating that he in no way believed me.

"I did, I did!" I added, thinking I must be sounding like Tweety Bird.

"I believe him," said a forty-something man behind me now standing at the Updater. "At our age we start to forget things like that."

"It's my fifty dollars," I said somewhat defiantly to the Brink's protestor. I stuck it in my pocket and headed for the door. Nobody chased me; the guard didn't even pull out his gun. My face was bright red before I cleared the door of the bank on No. 3 Road in Richmond, B.C. with its three automated teller machines and one automated bankbook updater. I wonder if the lists of services banks sell will ever include automatic personal mind recallers with foolish insurance?

When I was young my Dad sometimes called me "dense." He called me dense mostly when he'd sent me to the toolshed for a tool that he said would be lying on the workbench right in front of me when I stood facing it, but I just could never see it even after three trips to stare at the bench. How that tool got there in such plain view after he finally heaved himself up from under some piece of equipment, muttering, and went and looked himself amazed me. Still does.

I think Dad's description of dense described absentmindedness, not dullness. It meant that someone who was intelligent in most ways had suddenly turned out to be way below the average in some area of their lives.

On occasion, I get dense. My mind goes blank.

That's all there is to it. That's life; that's the human condition. And it seems to me these blanks increase in propensity as I grow older; it seems, too, they are increasing in frequency.

A friend of mine, an older and a wise friend, says that elderly people aren't forgetful because they're old, they just seem to be forgetful because it takes a long time to go through such a vast storehouse of information that they have built up from having lived so much.

In stark contrast to any such time created human blankness, however, is a timeless God, an ageless God, who is the same, yesterday, today and forever. God didn't forget anything yesteryear, so he won't forget anything next year.

The anti-theists, postmodern agnostics and age-old atheists think they can trip up theistic believers with the question, "If it is true that God made everything, who made God?" That question has an easy answer. "Nobody!" God has always been. If there was a time when God wasn't, then we're not talking about God. God has operated, operates and will operate outside of time, as we know it, and therefore always was and always will be, because he is God. God by very definition doesn't need a Maker of himself. That's how magnificent the God of Scripture and holy experience is, a God for everyday, who has always been everyday. A God who does not change; who does not lose it. A God who is steady and true and the ultimate insurance for those of us who are not and will not be as steady and as sharp as we once were. God always will be.

The Family

We convened as an extended family, over ninety of us. The purpose was to remember, reconnect and even reconstruct, as a clan. We played ball, went tubing on the rolling river, rode horses, roasted wieners over open fires, sang, shared meals and told stories.

As part of the organized and official stuff, I was given the job of leading some group conversation about "the family." I set the "patriarchs"—Peter, Frank, my dad Jacob, Henry—and their sister Helen in the front, in the center of what became a circle of rings of the subsequent generations. I knew well enough to begin the conversation around Uncle Pete, 86, the eldest. I asked him about the emigration from Russia 60 years ago, about the trip and the adjustment to life in Canada. His siblings, of course, soon chimed in, giving their interpretations of what the experience had been like, commenting on what was said, or disagreeing whenever it was deemed necessary. I didn't want facts, though, I wanted impressions and feelings. Watching the family dynamics in the interchange, the competition and the shifting allegiances and alliances of these retired but highly energized siblings, I finally found a rich entrance to a spirited conversation in which we could all participate.

"Do you ever stop being aware of who is the oldest, who is the youngest, who is the middle child, and so on, in a family this large, in a family that's stayed connected this long?" I asked.

"Oh, yes," said Aunt Helen, the leveler and peacemaker, the one always wanting everything to be calm and settled. "We've forgotten those things long ago!"

"Except when we were kids. Jake always had it the easiest. He always got to help Mom in the house and not do his chores in the barn!" stated Uncle Henry matter-of-factly but energetically.

"I did not!" retorted Jacob, "I had to do all my chores in the barn like the rest of you, and then help Mom and Helen with the housework while you just waited to be served!"

"Neither one of you had to work as hard as we older ones," shouted Frank as the energy of the conversations escalated and the pronouncements became louder. Uncle Pete, older and not as quick as the others any more, couldn't get a word in as the tempo and noise level of the argument continued to rise like a thermometer with the sun suddenly on it. The younger generations observing all this were stirred and brightened; they were stimulated and amused by the animation, the arguments and the disagreement of the old order.

At the back of the room, Jacob's son Jake, one of the older ones of the second generation, and also a leveler and peacemaker, was waving his arms like a football referee demanding that I, the facilitator, put an end to the fray. I think he thought this conflict was not appropriate, not right.

We let the thing run on a while, nevertheless, and

then took the discussion towards what it felt like to be part of this clan, starting with reflections by the older ones and ending with the younger generations. Finally the thing ended with the in-laws being questioned on their view of this clan they had gotten for free in the marriage deals they had brokered.

A couple of years later, my dad went to the Philippines. He was now 81. His brother Frank, 84, accompanied him. They had found some trip, a missionary gimmick some said, whereby the tour group members would work half days building a church and spend the rest of the day sightseeing the area around the community they were in. Dad and Frank, the most senior members of the group, and brothers, were assigned to each other as work partners.

A few days into their adventure, my dad called me in British Columbia from his temporary Philippine adventure. He was roaring. My dad roared very little in his life and I was impressed at his passion that day.

"I'm having some real trouble with Uncle Frank!" he shouted on the phone, demonstrating more agitation than I remembered him exhibiting even when I had walked with him, almost 30 years earlier, holding his hand, through a crop smashed to bits by golf ball-sized hailstones.

"What's the deal? What's he doing?" I asked.

"Well, he blacks out, you know!"

"No, I didn't know!"

"Yeah, it's happened a couple of times. He just sort of falls asleep for a second or so, when he's driving."

"But he's not driving there."

"No, that was at home, before. But now we're working together building. Carrying wet cement in ice-cream pails. We're pouring a new floor in the church."

"You two old guys carrying cement in ice-cream pails? Sounds like a rush job."

35

"Yeah!" he laughed. "But yesterday we were supposed to cut up some plywood with the Skil saw. I told
Frank, here, you hold the board and I'll cut it. He said,
No. I said, yes, you'll faint. You hold the board and I'll
cut it. And then, you know what he said? He said, big
brothers don't hold boards for little brothers to cut, it's
always the other way around. Well, I dropped the saw
right there. I don't care if that board ever gets cut."

A few weeks later the two old missionary carpenter
laborers came home, completely worn out. Dad com-
plained that the heavy exhaust fumes in the Philippine
streets had affected his breathing and caused him
chest pains. He didn't know, nor did we, that a dis-
eased heart was rapidly cutting him down.

Six months later a massive heart attack took his
earthly breath away forever, and the clan gathered to
pay its respects, to say farewell to Jacob, to remember,
to reconnect and to reconstruct. All good things to do
when a family system has been invaded by death.

We met in the viewing room at the funeral home.
The place smelled of chrysanthemums and other funeral flowers. Dad's body lay in state in an open coffin. We cried a little, talked in hushed tones at first,
and finally began reminiscing. The stories rose and
fell and minutes turned into an hour and more.

Suddenly, in a gap of silence, Uncle Pete, the oldest
brother, the natural born leader, raised himself to his
shaky feet and shuffled his 89-yeared body forward towards the open coffin. His leathery old face was con-
torted in pain. His voice hoarse with age, still thick
with an old-country accent, he stammered, "Jacob, you
should not have died before me!" And he wept for his
departed brother and for his own loss. It was easy to
see a kind of survivor's guilt washing over him.

Even in death, the birth order is violated when
someone in the family steps out of sequence.

"Everything has its time and place!" Who said that? Probably everyone who has lived into adulthood. And yet because any number of violations of every sort of law occur all the time, could it not be possible that the laws of space and time also get disturbed every once in a while?

When a child dies before her parent, or a younger sibling predeceases his older siblings, the survivors are doubly devastated by the death. Why? Because we have come to believe that everything has its time and place, and in the untimely death of a younger person the survivors feel themselves caught in a grave violation. Birth order, we unconsciously think, must determine death order. And then the order twists and reverses itself. My dad, Jacob, didn't die on purpose, of course, but his elder siblings double felt their loss at his death because they felt it should not have happened at all in their lifetime.

We humans want order, we need order. God, in spite of the world's disorder caused mostly by our human free-spiritedness and fallenness, is a God of order. Our days are orderly in indescribably deep ways when we invite him to order our spirit and our attitudes and our ways. And the order he gives relates to what is at our center, our spirit, in spite of outward disorder. God has a wonderful uncanny way of settling waves, making them manageable even as the storm continues.

The Photographer

He was a friend of the family. How he first became part of our "affection circle" I never found out, but from the beginning we always knew him to be a humorous and delightful man. The infrequent family photo sessions demanded by mother, and grumbled about by the rest of us, were always punctuated with laughter prompted by the hilarity of the photographer. Some private shoots with him around special events and special groups proved to be congenial occasions. One would have thought this classy clown had lived a free and easy life; that he had never encountered anything to cloud his demeanor. Such was not the case, however. Over time I learned his story.

Many of the photographer's ethnic brothers and sisters and forebears had shaken the dust of Russia off their feet in the 1920s, leaving for the relative freedoms and excesses of lands to the west. Somehow he had stayed behind. The photographer lived in Russia through the difficult inter-war years under the horrific leadership of Josef Stalin, married and had a child as the war raged. When the war ended and German nationals could leave Russia more easily than before, the photographer made plans with his little family to get out.

Finally they were at the train station, their belongings packed in rough suitcases and boxes or tied up in sheets and bundles. The teeming train platform, crushed with far more humanity than the platform had room for, was a frightening maelstrom for the young photographer-artist and his wife, now pregnant. His young son, nearly trampled, was crying, feeling terror. The mass of people pushing, shoving and shouting, and the easily perceived anxiety of his parents horrified him.

Somehow this little family band, holding hands in and around all the belongings they were desperately trying not to get separated from, got disconnected in the crazy crowd of travelers, thieves, soldiers and sellers. The photographer was suddenly without his family. Frantically he shouted, "Maria! Maria! David!" No one would ever hear above this noise. Retracing steps against the mass of sweating, shoving bodies trying to get on the train, the photographer could find no trace of his wife and child. Then the train started to move. The human mass convulsed toward the train. People screamed. Policemen blew whistles; conductors swore. The photographer elbowed and bullied his way up the nearest steps onto the now moving train, half swimming and mauling his way through the other bodies, thinking, hoping, praying that his wife had fought her way onto the train with their little boy.

As the train picked up speed, leaving behind those who could not squeeze on, the photographer started his search, along the overcrowded, already stuffy and soon unhygienic length of the train. He felt a little anxious, but he was relieved to be travelling and his imagination did not conjure up the image of his little family back on the platform, a homeless pregnant woman with a tearful boy waiting for a husband and a dad who must have gotten on the train without them. The platform was almost empty of people now and he was not there. As the abandoned family waited on the platform, the photographer kept working his way along the train thinking he would soon find them. By the time he had reached the end of the train the first time, it was raining back at the decrepit Russian railway station where his family waited. A passer-by would have seen a pregnant woman sobbing and holding onto a little boy, crying as if she had no idea which way to go, or how to get there.

Working his way back and forth along the whole length of the lurching train, over and over, the photographer began to realize his family might not be on it. Slowly the awareness that he was miles and miles away from them at the station made itself known in his consciousness. By this time, too, the train was close to the border and close to "getting out" of the country. There was no way back. Like his son in the rain so many miles away, the photographer started to cry, leaning his head against a lurching and steamed-up window of the train. He could not go back. There was no way back.

The photographer followed the immigrant refugee route he and his wife had so much talked about, across the tense and dangerous border, through seamless grey days and dark nights, feeling lonely and guilty and angry. Angry with himself; angry with the Communists. The formerly laughing jokester now spoke only when he had to. He almost never smiled anymore; he carried himself like a man depressed. He couldn't quite remember, later, how he got on the ship and made passage to Canada. He remembered just a grey numbness and blurred shadows of people, officials and other refugees. But weeks, or was it months, later, he unpacked the few things he had clutched in a cloth bag through the journey to his new country and began scheming, between finding shelter, food and work, to find a way to reach his family. In the same week that he unpacked his few possessions, among them an increasingly precious and crinkled picture of his wife, the borders of Russia slammed shut and his letters to possible addresses were either returned or disappeared without response.

The photographer set up a studio and became a Canadian photographer. While photographing families with small children some of the twinkle in his eyes came back, and as his heartache and loneliness became normal, some of his old charming spirit slowly returned. Meanwhile, he kept mailing letters to every Russian village imaginable where he thought his wife might be. The response was always an empty mailbox, no letters, no word. Every day he looked at the picture of his wife and wondered and worried about the birth, the boy. Were they alive? Were they well? Were they...? He wouldn't allow himself to imagine the worst.

A year passed. The photographer took out some pencils, and looking at his wife's fading photo, sketched her as he imagined she might look now. Another year, another sketch. Every year he sketched another portrait of her, making her a year older, imagining her face, the lines of her lips, the arch of her cheekbones, the soft bristle of her eyebrows, the curl of her hair escaping from under a kerchief one year, or tightly pulled back from her face another. He put the growing progression on the wall of his photo studio. Those who saw the drawings could see that the photographer was aging his wife along with himself.

Finally the fifties came and in 1953 Josef Stalin, the ruthless Peter the Great of modern Russia, died. Nikita Khruschev became Premier of the Soviet Union and the world held its breath to see whether this short, rotund, sometimes jovial man would be at the very least a little more humane than his Soviet predecessor.

One day in 1959 in a little photo studio in southern Manitoba, the photographer read in the *Winnipeg Free Press* that the normally reclusive yet Cold-warring and aggressive Russians were sending their leader, Nikita Khruschev, to New York to address the United Nations. The day he read the news, the photographer hurried out, bought a bus ticket and left for New York. With the motivation of years of pain and separation, he found out what hotel Khruschev was staying at, and set up a vigil against a restraining rope meant to hold back the crowds, crazies and gawkers from coming too close to the entrance. The second morning of his vigil, as the photographer stood watching and waiting, a line of limousines rolled up to the magnificent building. Something important was about to happen. The hotel lobby, which the photographer could see through the huge brass and glass doors, was filling with serious-looking men in dark coats and hats. Someone of importance was about to appear. Would he actually get to see the man he had come to see? Suddenly Premier Khruschev was in the lobby. He was rounder and surprisingly shorter than the photographer had expected. (Famous people are almost always smaller than we imagine them to be.) The Soviet leader headed for the spinning doors. Security men a head taller jostled around him, watching the crowds. The entourage moved briskly through the doorway past the uniformed doormen, heading to the waiting cars.

"That's some country you run, Secretary Khruschev!," shouted the photographer in Russian. "I write letters to your country and I get no responses. Don't you have any systems that work in that Mother Russia of ours?" He stressed the "ours", pushing for identification.

The Soviet leader stopped and looked around to see who was shouting in Russian, a button pushed by the criticism of his responsibility. He scanned the not so small group of faces at the rope. The crowd hushed. Khruschev moved toward the rope. Now he could see who was shouting at him. The photographer held his ground. The bodyguards became agitated and apprehensive with Khruschev's move towards the crowd. Khruschev, himself, stung a little, and not used to open criticism was shrewd enough, however, to know how to turn an electric moment into a public relations victory. "Where are you from, comrade?" he asked quietly. "What seems to be the problem? You write letters to whom?"

The photographer spilled out his story of his separation at the train station so many years ago, and his hopeful belief that his wife and children were still alive somewhere in the Soviet Union. He wrote her name on a piece of paper, and not so gently again scolded the Premier for being so paranoid that mail went undelivered, for keeping families apart and for the systems failing to have any sense of human decency. The Russian leader seemed genuinely interested and seemed not to notice the criticism. Amazingly, he promised to look into the matter as soon as he got home. Khruschev handed the photographer's slip of paper with its precious name to one of his aides. The photographer stood breathless as Khruschev swung away from him and headed briskly to his waiting car.

Thunderstruck by the encounter and overwhelmed by the emotion of just having told his painful story to the most powerful man of the Soviet Union, the photographer felt his knees weaken. Somewhat dazed, he retraced his steps to the station from which he could begin his trip back to his home, virtually unaware of where he was going, thinking only of what had happened and fantasizing about what might come of it. The photographer laughed and he cried. Emotions of all kinds rose and fell in his spirit and showed on his face.

Back in his studio a few days later, the photographer started working on the next drawing of his wife. The pictures made a striking eight-inch by ten-inch border along the top of the wall of the studio now. Soon three weeks had passed. The photographer wondered about all that had transpired. He relived the brief conversation with Khruschev over and over. He didn't know how many times he had told the story of his Khruschev meeting to those interested and those willing to listen, but already he was wondering what he should have said differently.

Then one Tuesday, following his daily schedule, the photographer slipped on his coat and walked to get the mail from the post office, chatting good naturedly, as always, with the cronies and regulars who visited in the post office vestibule with bundles of mail in their hands. The photographer noticed an envelope in his bundle of bills and notices that was made of darker, cheaper paper. He quickly turned it over. In an instant he saw the Russian markings, and his heart skipped to see his name in a tight and pointed indelible pencil scrawl that seemed vaguely familiar. He ripped open the envelope, "My dear Henry, I have found you...." The photographer fell to his knees in the post office in a scream-shout that commingled all the emotions known to humankind: a mourning for all those lost years and an outpouring of the joy of family found, of hoped-for reconciliation. It was said that in that moment, the photographer expressed more emotion than all the people in this mostly Teutonic town had expressed in public in a whole generation. He got up and rushed home to his studio. Preparations would need to be made.

He knew it would be some months before the red-tape could be cleared and the arrangements made for his wife and their two children, now mostly grown up, to come to Canada. Months dragged into years, but finally the Russian threesome passed through Customs and into the arms of the photographer, a husband and a father. A man who through his longsuffering loneliness never gave up. It was a greeting almost too sacred to watch as these four people, shyly exuberant, laughed and cried their welcome, their greeting to one another, really dancing together a celebration of family. A wife much remembered, a little boy now a man who couldn't remember his dad, and a daughter who was born after the terrible day on the train platform so long ago.

A few weeks later a new photograph was mounted on the wall in the photo studio. The new photo of the smiling photographer's wife, newly come to Canada, and reunited with her husband after two decades of separation became the end piece, the exclamation mark at the end of the long row of portrait sketches. The thing was done, the picture completed, the broken circle repaired and closed.

As I write this reflection I haven't seen my wife and children for a month. But in that time I've talked to them on the phone three times and I've had nearly daily contact through electronic means of communication. Never were they lost to me, never did I wonder whether they were in friendly or in hostile surroundings. Besides that knowing, the plan was that after a month and a few days we would reunite as a family in an international airport in an exotic part of the world, excitement and intrigue adding to the joy of family being together again.

In the meantime though, in the separation, my life is decidedly unreal. No children to read to, no taxi-ing of teens to school and youth events, no shouting to "get off the phone," no arguments to referee, no wonderful day's-end de-briefings with a spouse to "keep in touch," body, soul and spirit. I can go to bed when I am tired, I can get up when I am rested, I am not directly responsible for anyone for all these days. I am like a sailing ship without wind, really. I get lots of work done. I think, I walk, I write and I make conversations with strangers, dozens and dozens of strangers, but there is no closeness, no touching. I am a man in a daze. But this is not a tragedy in the making, for it will end with a reuniting.

The photographer lived what Thomas Hardy wrote about in his novels: near misses, human tragedies that could have so easily been avoided but weren't. But the story is about more than that. The story is about a hope that never dies. A determination that keeps running up the hill that one rolls back down every day for years and years, and then whose summit is finally reached. In this story come together all human pain and all human joy.

God is so often yelled at by those who say they don't believe in him because if he was "up there" how could he stand by and let all the human losses the world is full of play themselves out. Who are they yelling at? God sent his son to die for us, a death that coagulated every horror known to humans, and God stood and let it happen. God knows what loss is. And when, three days in eternity later, the stone slid open on a man mysteriously, miraculously raised from death to life again, the epitome of hope, life coming back after death, good news following bad news, delight dancing out of horror, we begin to grasp what God is like over time. God knows loss beyond our nightmares and horrific imaginings, but God is higher than that, he is about hope. He is about reconciliation, the ultimate reconciliation that will bring together all that is best beyond time, space and experience. That's the kind of God to link onto as one soars or runs or walks or crawls or is carried through life. The best is yet to come.

The Goodbye People

Jacob had often talked about spouses not releasing their loved ones who were dying. He recalled the sheer agony of having watched a dying relative enduring massive misery while waiting for her partner to catch up to the reality, to make some peace with the emotional place of letting go. "I'm not doing that!" Jacob said. "When my Mary needs to die, when it's her time, she should not have to wait for me to let her go!"

Jacob tenderly cared for Mary through months of intensely serious illness after many years of varying ill health. They had been married for 50 years and more, and the bulk of their memories were good. The financially tough years on low-income farms had not been able to sear the good memories of their marriage. They could recall good and tough times regardless of relative poverty or relative wealth. Their relationship and its manifestations was about something far more and much other than money, possessions and income. Their relationship had centered itself around children, community, a shared faith, shared to-

getherness and problem solving, not around the depth
or the weight of the problems they had faced.

Many days in that last year when morphine took
away Mary's ability to talk, or even think the way she
wanted to be able to in her hospital bed, we noticed a
new and wonderful day's end ritual between the two
old lovers who knew the days of their marriage were almost done. Just before saying goodbye for the night,
after keeping vigil all day, Jacob would lean down over
Mary and, placing his face very close to hers, would intensely whisper his goodnight words to her. Even if
she hadn't opened her eyes all day, suddenly now she
would open them and just as passionately as he, would
respond to him. The energy that flowed between
them was almost visible. Those of us in the room, or
at the door, would almost feel like we were intruding,
or watching something too intimate, too private, too
sacred to be a part of. We children would often step
out of the hospital room as this relational exchange
between the two aging lovers played itself out.

One day, after seeing this wonderful and intense
connection between the two, I asked Jacob, "This in-
tensity, this love, this energy between you two. Has it
always been there?"

"You finally noticed!" he said. Proudly, I think.

But her days in the hospital grew in agony for Mary.
Soon Jacob was at her side for most of her days and
her nights.

I lived three hours drive away from them and needing to bring closure to something, I drove the three
hours out to the little hospital where Mary lay dying,
and where Jacob lived out his caregiving with hands
and words. I arrived at Mary's hospital bedside just after noon one weekday and found them pleasantly and
quite comfortably talking and filling the day with news
and chatter. Mary was having a good day. Their talk

these days often turned quite matter-of-factly toward Mary's impending death. Though she appeared to be doing well this particular day, her strength was rapidly diminishing.

With the three of us, I on one side of the bed and Jacob standing shotgun on the other, I asked the question, "So, do you two talk about saying goodbye here, or is it too hard? Do you pretend that this will just go on forever?"

Jacob looked sharply at me, wondering, I guess, whether I was teasing or serious about the issue of death and leave-taking.

"No, we talk about it," he said. Mary didn't say anything, her look was thoughtful. She couldn't raise her head off the pillow any more.

"Let me take over for a while, Dad," I volunteered. "You go home and have a rest, or go for a round of golf or something. I can stay for a few hours."

He sighed, not wanting to go, but finally agreed. "Mom and I were just going to pray before you came," he said. "We'll do that now and then I'll go home for a while." Jacob laid his hands over Mary's hands folded together at her waist, and he started, in German, "Dear heavenly Father. We thank you for this day. We thank you for all the things you give us. Your blessings. Your help. Mary, here, is sick and she is suffering." He stopped, sniffling a little, " and, Father, don't let her suffer too much. When it is her time, before she suffers too much, take her home. I give her up to you. Take her home. Get her ready. I release her to you, O greater God! Amen!" He wept, his aged eyes tightly shut and closed within their pockets of seventy-five-year wrinkles of laughing, living and squinting on windswept steppes and prairies and dazzling white snowdrifted winters.

Mary seemed calm, even serene. She let him cry

silently for a moment or two, and then she prayed, in English, "God, you are God! You may take me home now. My work is finished. My Jacob has given me to you, now I give myself to you. Take me home, Lord. I am ready. Amen!" A little tear escaped from a corner of her eye, but her prayer seemed natural, almost commonplace. Like something one does when one is near death.

Several days later she was gone. Released by her husband, released by herself, and finally released from her suffering. All the farewells had been said.

How do we say Goodbye? Is it possible to really say, Fare thee well!? We say goodbye for a few days, a few weeks or months, but forever? How does one do that? I have often wondered what it must have been like for my parents and grandparents, and millions of others down through history, to say goodbye to family members when they left Russia or other places. Travelling in those years wasn't nearly as easy as it is now; trips were almost always only one way.

Is it possible to "bless" someone and say "goodbye" at the same time? Maybe that's what makes saying goodbye possible—blessing the other, wishing that person the absolute best for the rest of her days. That blessing doesn't take away the pain of separation but it opens the channels of love to flow between the two saying farewell. The answer then, to being able to say goodbye in the best meaning of that word, is to bless, to bestow goodness and happiness and God's hand upon the departing one. Jacob and Mary were saying goodbye but the exchange became manageable, even spiritually magical, because the conduit of love between the two, and their connectedness to their God

51

at the same time, was without interference, and hence, the experience was warm and peaceful. Tearful, yes, but acceptable and graceful and even serene.

God is in the business of blessing those who seek his blessing. He forces himself on no one, but those who don't ask, who don't pursue, nor "follow hard after him" simply miss the blessing. In missing God's blessing, we miss the ability to have clear lines of exchange with others and certainly with God. As a result goodbyes are wrenching, they are a violation, a tragedy. Every day God wants to bless his people, those who simply reach out in acknowledgement to him. Among the abilities that flow out of this is the ability to say goodbye in tranquillity.

Alexei

He squeezed into the too narrow El Al airliner seat beside me, mumbling his mostly unfriendly apologies to me in Hebrew, assuming that I understood him. I had tried to help him by moving the seat belt and pillow off his seat so he could sit down more easily. He gruffly waved off my help. He sat stiffly beside me. I sensed tension, even more than tension. He stared straight ahead at the brocaded seat protector hanging over the airplane seat ahead of him. Nothing about his demeanor invited conversation, in fact, it warned it off.

Once or twice in the first hours of the flight he took to standing in the aisle with so many of the other passengers. Unlike the others, though, who were praying, bobbing into their prayer books, visiting, arguing about great truths that had for many centuries already been discussed, helping themselves to drinks in the galley, or just moving up and down the overcrowded aisle, he stood sternly, staring nowhere. On one of his nervous sorties from his seat into the aisle, his movements jerky as a caged animal, he slipped into the claustrophobic washroom and came out wearing a different set of clothes. His shirt was buttoned tightly up to the top. Above his collar his Adam's apple tortured itself as he swallowed nervously, incessantly. He meticulously folded his jacket and the other clothes he had changed out of and arranged them neatly in the plane's overhead compartment. Before seating himself again, he stood outside the galley carefully staring at no one, brooding, it seemed. Every time he took his seat next to me I tried some gentle kindness to ease his sitting, trying to find an opening to talk to this man who was either terribly afraid of flying or in some other kind of deep distress.

I guessed that this airplane, which today resembled a human sardine can, didn't add any comfort to this experience, but my efforts at wordless connection seemed only to annoy him. To the flight attendant he spoke Hebrew, but the book he was reading on smart investments was written in English. Finally I braved a comment.

"You are Israeli?" I used the sentence structure and even the tone of the Hebrew language.

"Yes," he answered.

"And you have been visiting in Canada?"

"Yes, my children are in Canada. In Montreal." He scowled, his face clouded over.

"They live in Canada? Had you not seen them for awhile?"

"No, they moved from Israel some years ago and they will not come back." His attitude signaled he did not want to talk anymore. I slipped into silence. He locked his eyes again into the back of the seat in front of him.

Moments, maybe even half an hour, passed. I thought he might want me to speak again, but nothing moved. His hands lay folded in his lap. In my sidelong glances I saw deep unrest, possibly even sadness. Finally he picked up his book again, but he didn't read.

"You speak Hebrew, but I see that you read in English," I commented. "My name is Danny."

"And my name is Alexei," he volunteered, a little warmth showing in his eyes. "Yes, it speaks easily for me in Hebrew, but it is easier for me to read in English. I was not born in Israel; I was born in Russia."

"Ah! And where are you living in Israel? How long have you been?" I prodded.

"In Haifa. I came to Israel from Russia so that my children could be raised and live in Israel and now they want nothing of it. They are living in Montreal with Chinese and Indian and French friends. They are assimilated. They want nothing of Israel. The youngest boy even did not do his military service; he cannot come back to Israel. They make no difference with their friends. They are from all different peoples and they just make a life together, running to clubs, spending money. I don't understand."

"Did you stay with your sons?"

"Yes, I stayed with them. But it did not go so good. I am an old man. I cannot run with them in the night and go to their places."

"You have great pain around your sons!" I risked.

"Yes! But what can I do?

"Did you argue with them?"

"Yes, but let us say that we have agreed to disagree."

"Have you lost your relationship with them? Will you visit them again?"

"Yes, I hope. No, the relation is not broken but it is tense. It is sad. A father should have good relations with his sons, and the sons should consider the wishes of their father. I am discouraged."

"What was your relationship with your father?"

55

"It was very distant. We hardly talked. He was so stiff."

"Did you keep a relationship with him?"

"Yes! No! Hardly!"

"Is that why you want so much to stay connected with your sons, to, in a manner of speaking, atone for the past?"

"No, I just want my boys to do what is right. This is very painful for me!"

It seemed to me that in spite of his pain, maybe because of it, Alexei could not see that what his father had done with him, he was doing with his sons; what he had done, his sons were doing. Could he not see that their sons, too, would probably repeat what they were doing in relationship to their father?

"Do you think, then, that it was a mistake to leave Russia and come live in Israel?"

"No, that was not a mistake. It is a mistake that my boys live in Montreal."

"Do you say that for religious reasons? Are you religious and your boys have decided not to be?"

"No, we were never religious. The religion has nothing to do with it. I just always thought that my sons would be a part of Israel. But what can one do?"

The distressed man closed his eyes and pulled the airplane blanket neatly folded up from his lap, over his chest and up to his chin. He shivered as if he were cold. The cabin was warm and stuffy. Children played and cried; passengers four and five rows apart shouted to one another. The cabin crew, looking road weary, half-heartedly tried to keep some order to the flight.

Movies one after another rolled by, their images dancing on screens hanging from the plastic ceilings. Hebrew subtitles teased and dared those who had once studied bits of biblical Hebrew to attempt the

56

words, sound out the letters, guess at the missing vowels.

Alexei slept. Or he hid from his interrogator behind closed eyes.

Suddenly the plane dropped off an invisible air cliff and bounced through unseen but deep and disturbing ruts of rough air. Passengers in the aisles lost their balance and reached out to steady themselves in the lurching plane. The flight attendants, happy, I think, for the natural justification, herded all the pitching wanderers back to their seats, who, for the first time needed no convincing.

Alexei turned to me, his eyes large in his darkly tanned sixtyish face, "You are from Canada, no?"

"Yes!" I answered.

"Is there respect for fathers and their ways in your country?" And without waiting for an answer, he added, "I think the world is changing. And not to something better."

The darkness outside the windows of the plane weakened, as soft morning light gradually transformed the night. Alexei shook himself; now he seemed warmer, friendlier. The plane started to descend.

Excitement at being on the sacred ground, at getting off this plane, at having the journey ended, stirred the passengers. We busied ourselves to get ready to disembark in the next half hour. Alexei next to me made small conversation about taking a taxi to Haifa and asked about my plans for the next few days.

As the plane landed, he became intense again, and then in the standing aisles, once we were safely on the ground and waiting for the doors to free us, Alexei reached out, shook my hand, and wished me "Shalom!"

"And I wish you Shalom too, Alexei" I responded. "I hope you can make peace with your sons. It will be what they really want, too." Alexei smiled for the first time. A dream-like look took over his face, and he was gone.

A lexei was hurt. Hurt by the separation, the gulf between himself and his sons. Alexei was a man in mourning. His pain seemed insatiable, inconsolable. There seemed no way for him to feel any comfort or even to consider hope. He saw his sons disappearing into the night of a foreign culture without any of the values that he, their father, thought were absolutely integral to living well, to living as one should.

It was encouraging to me to see the break in his demeanor when I quite innocently and without much thought said that I thought his boys would want a mended and an intimate relationship with him, too. Somewhere in that statement a hopeful button got pushed, and Alexei experienced, in a second, the joy of what it would feel like to be full-hearted with his sons.

God is the reconciler of relationships; his son Jesus came to walk the barren and rocky hills of Palestine to make the ultimate reconciliation for humankind, and in that aftermath came the ability to live in hope and in the reality of human reconciliation in all directions. Every day, the God of reconciliation mourns our broken relationships and smiles when we can find ways to mend misunderstandings, put away pettiness, unfurl some forgiveness, and jettison that plain old stupidity that stalks our lives if we let it. The sparkle that came into Alexei's eyes at the thought of being "whole" with his boys was the smile of God's image in a man whose life is weary and pained beyond what the Creator wants for anyone.

Aref

We walked stiffly through the "now at peace" no-man's land between Israel and Jordan, two modern nation-states and traditional enemies at last trying to co-exist. We felt the tension that lives in the air above all border crossings, no matter how friendly or dangerous. Borders, after all, exist to separate people, and we wondered whether a day at a luxury hotel poolside mightn't have been just a little easier than this. But we followed the arrows painted on the sidewalk; showed our passports to two or three guards before a thirtyish man in civilian clothes stopped us. He inquired as to our names and hearing what he was listening for, introduced himself as Aref, our arranged-for guide.

Aref stepped us through some of the details of the border crossing, speaking his Arabic with the border officials in tones we would describe as yelling. Whether he was arguing or just conversing with them, we could not tell. There would be more that we wondered about our guide this day. In less than an hour, however, we were through the border crossing and boarding a clean Mercedes mini-bus. The driver turned the bus towards the red mountains of the Trans-Jordanian range and we pulled into the smoky black exhaust traffic of modern day Jordan—mostly trucks hauling goods and crude oil from the port of Aqaba to the exotic-sounding cities of Amman and Baghdad and even beyond. Truck upon truck, a convoy of trucks, carrying on a centuries old convoying tradition in this region, navigated the snake-like road up through the mountain passes, a slow moving journey as we entered canyons of rock faces and scree washes without bush, tree or living green anywhere. Dry riverbeds called wadis winding down the mountains, provided some basis for the rare sparse bushes with faint green coloring if one looked carefully enough or had a green imagination.

Aref, microphone in hand, weaved the story of modern Jordan around geographic and geologic facts, political smoke and mirrors regarding Israel and the United States and Arab world perceptions. His words were laced with veiled and unveiled messages of hope and pessimism, as he moved us into his version of Nabatean history and Bedouin folklore.

After a stop in an ancient Jordanian village boasting a watering place that the villagers purported to be the rock that spewed its water out after Moses struck it with his staff thousands of years before in a Bible story, we headed for Petra. Petra, famous lost city of the Nabateans, wealthy trader Bedouins of myrrh and masters of thousands of camel caravans traipsing from the southern Arabian deserts to Mediterranean ports in centuries gone by, beckoned us with its magic. We clambered out of our bus and stepped into the company of sellers and hucksters. We spurned the invitations to ride the little Arabian tourist horses into the Petra site, which the Jordanians call their oil, due to their not having any "liquid black gold" themselves unlike their rich Arab neighbor states, and the money its tourism brings. We entered on foot a high narrow fissure slashed into the red rock of a mountain. Towering hundreds of feet on both sides of us, the curved walls sometimes only three to five meters apart overshadowed us as we walked the ancient pavements of a mysterious and exotic lost civilization. Aref tossed out gentle snippets of history and pointed out to us relief carvings of camels and their drivers and prayer and worship sites carved into the rock faces that the untrained eye would not see. More than 800 burial caves, magnificent temples towering over a hundred feet high and nearly as wide, took our breath away as they appeared around curves in the canyon. No wonder Hollywood gravitates to this place to shoot movies whose fictions could never be as fantastic as the real stories that have played out here over thousands of years. Bedouin children, gentler and less insistent than their Arab cousins in the streets of Old Jerusalem, tried to interest us in buying necklaces, stones in magnificent orange and blue hues, and clear glass bottles of multicolored sands in layers with whatever name you wish inscribed in a sand of its own color. We wound our way around rock faces and through open spaces following Aref and listening as he teased us with no more detail than we could absorb in this exotic place.

Rounding one corner far below a precipice topped by the ruin of a Crusader fortress (whose history should make Christians red-faced for the legacy they have left for Muslims and Jews to remind us of), we stood before a marvelous house carved out of multi-hued red, orange and blue rock surrounded by dashes of brilliant, waist high flowers. Just as Aref started to tell us that the owner of this house, a Bedouin who had received special permission from King Hussein to live here in Petra, came out and greeted us. Below his red checkered *jabilah* and through his broad brown sun-baked smile revealing missing teeth, he beamed out his hospitality. He lit a cigarette with a silver lighter. The blonde women in our group were enthusiastically invited to "see his house." As we moved on, Aref told us that this Bedouin "king" had one wife in Switzerland and another in Holland, their wifely responsibility requiring that they spend only one month a year with him in his rocky palace. Children of his Bedouin wives lived in an encampment not so far away. By this time we didn't know whether we were part of a movie script or whether we were locked in some kind of ethereal dream or hallucinational trip induced by the mountain air or the bromide from the Dead Sea down the western side of this mountain that can make its visitors giggly.

The heat, the dust and mundane hunger reminded us of our realities and we stopped under a reed-roofed, wall-less enclosure housing a Bedouin cafeteria complete with stainless steel containers with a wide variety of hot dishes, plates of colorful fresh fruits and vegetables, white-shirted waiters and Pepsi dispensers. A quiet Bedouin boy of twelve or thirteen informed us we could also enjoy a prepared cold lunch of pita bread with meat and cheese, tomatoes, cucumbers, yogurt, cookies and an egg for five dollars, if that's what we preferred. Aref took our orders and mediated our needs with our servers as we rested our eyes, our spirits and our experience meters from the exotic overload. Two members of our group took instructions on how to scale higher reaches of the mountain for more rock-face carving extravaganza as the rest of us lingered with Aref over our simple lunch made particularly delicious because our senses had been extended by this day and everything about it.

Aref chatted about his two wives, his three young sons and his being exempted from his daily prayers to Allah that day because he was more than a hundred kilometers away from his home, on the proviso that he do double prayers tomorrow. Our tour completed and his storytelling done, Aref and I retraced our steps to the parking lot two or three kilometers away through the fissure. He talked. He talked of extremists in his religion violating the teachings of Mohammed through violence and the killing of women and children, pointing out that the desert code and its religion is more about hospitality and brotherhood than anything else. "A few extremists are giving us a bad name, a bad reputation. Like your Christian crusaders and your TV preachers have done to you," he smiled. "We know that those crusaders, killing and maiming and leaving unborn children behind in every village they passed through, were not real Christians. Neither are those preachers who beg for money and have huge mansions, and neither are those extremists you read about in the newspapers real Muslims. Also, most of the rest of the Muslims who say they are true believers are not either, they are mostly secular, as are most of the people in your part of the world who say they are Christian, though their religion makes no difference to their living. Our faith, and your faith, I think," he continued, "are really heart faiths that are mostly about loving God and loving one's neighbor, are they not? In the behavior of too many people and some very high profile leaders, and I don't need to mention the name of your neighboring President, is a large moral emptiness. Societies that have no morals die. Where are the Nabateans today? We can't find them as a group. Where are the Greeks? The Romans who made this road? The Byzantine monks who worshipped here after the Nabateans were gone? Where will the powerful

nations of today be in some years? They are commit-
ting suicide through their immorality." He stopped his
accented but very articulate monologue, as if to breathe
in some silence and collect his impressions and fears
and frustrations and joys.

"I feel that you are my brother on this walk," he
said, his shift in subject surprising me, "although we
are of different faiths. I believe that what you and I
want is the same: peace with our brothers, respect with
our families, enough food and a good place to sleep."

We boarded our bus and in reflective silence most
of the way, drove back down the winding Jordanian
road of roaring trucks, through blowing sand drifting
across the road like Canadian snow, between moon-
like mountains spearing up out of miles of sand, past
clusters of inhabited goat-hair Bedouin tents. Aref
pointed out the concrete government-built houses
standing next to a number of the tents, but used mostly to house the nomads' animals. "After all, a cement
house isn't as climate controlled as a goat hair tent
whose fibers swell when it rains to keep out the water,
but lets in the cool breezes of the night. And when a
tent blows down its roof won't kill you." He smiled.

Aref barked some orders to our driver and the driver turned his bus off the road and up to the front
door of a roadside building. "How many waters do
you want? Two? Three?" He stepped off the bus and
came back carrying three liter bottles of water, their la-
bels sporting an outline of one of the Petra Temples.
"It's on me," he said as he passed out the bottles. We
continued our journey down through the mountain
pass that was reminiscent of a Rocky Mountain pass if
there were no trees or water in the riverbeds, toward
the tongue-end of the Gulf of Eilat and its uneasy-
peace city neighbors of Aqaba and Eilat.

As we approached the border, Aref collected our passports, asking each of us to place our American six-dollar "exit fee" in each official booklet. We passed one or two checkpoints, pulled up to a building, and as we waited, Aref disappeared around a corner with our passports and our money. He returned a few minutes later with our passports, minus the dollars now, and said, "I must leave you now. Your driver will take you to the Israeli gate." As I pressed a wad of American bills into his hand, a group tip expected and gladly given, Aref said a polite, "Thank you!" His eyes seemed distant and far away again I thought, as if he had something else preoccupying his mind, as if the magic of Petra was still blowing its winds through his spirit. And he was gone.

The bus took us another hundred meters and dropped us off at the Israeli controlled line. We walked through the gate, perspiring in the furnace-like heat, touched by something new, mystified by something inexplicable and somehow changed. How changed? Someday we might know.

And Aref? A rare gem, I think. He lives in Amman. He said we should visit him someday; we countered his invitation with ours to him. We exchanged cards. I can picture him standing at my door one day when I open it. Red dust will be blowing past him. It will be my turn to be host. Some of my ways will be mysterious to him.

A ref, our Jordanian guide, was a man who lived behind a mask. I felt warmth and affection in snatches from him in that long, short day we spent together, between the moments of distance and even coolness that he reflected towards me. When he talked of his faith, his country, his King, the uneasy peace with Israel, Saddam Hussein or other Arab neighbors, I could not tell whether he was telling things he wanted me to believe, whether he was trying to convince himself to believe, or whether he thought himself to be telling the facts.

When we cross the line between cultures we often don't see the invisible lines of differing mindsets, worldviews, language and thinking. We may be fluent in foreign languages, but it takes longer to understand how people in dissimilar cultures think differently than we do. But they are only as different from us as we are from them. And sometimes cultural presuppositions and more, simply don't translate.

Aref talked words at me. I think in some fleeting moments I caught glimpses of his heart, his hopes and his hurts, but the rest of his conversation was articulated for my benefit to learn and understand a little of what I was seeing. What he said that day, while fascinating, wasn't that important. What his heart and soul were doing behind those words is what makes up the man, Aref. I was intrigued by his mystery. I wanted to know who the man behind those dark, intelligent eyes and shrewd understanding really was. But a day is too short; a lifetime wouldn't be much longer.

Life is full of stuff we don't know. What makes my e-mail messages travel round the world in seconds? Why did I fall in love with whom I did, when I did? How intriguing that the wonderful children born to us might easily, in a millisecond of time, have been another one of the million other possibilities in personality, gifts, looks and so on.

But the mysteries we encounter, the stuff we don't know, are not beyond the scope of the God who made us and everything around us. The unknowingness of this world is not beyond God. We need not fret that nobody is minding the house. God is minding the house and he is not letting it crash and burn. He is watching it closely hour by hour, day by day, every day.

DR

DR is a Hollywood actor. And an artist with gifts and skills in color, texture and words, an artist with an extraordinary imagination and creativity to match. His audience is growing.

DR hails from stern stock. His Mennonite grandfather was strictly religious and religiously austere, but his father paved the way for DR to reject the tragedy of his joyless legalistic legacy and Grandpa's dour dogma, calling it all "dogmuck!"

We found a collection of DR's artwork and works of prose and poetry in an expensive, glossy coffee-table book.

A friend of mine, an art collector, was interested in buying some of DR's art, and I felt I'd like to talk with DR about the spirituality—his own brand—that seemed to be emerging from the ashes of his genealogy. He would probably say he has moved beyond anything resembling his grandfather's religion, but that influence, I think, hangs about much of his art. So I scoured the coffee-table book for clues to where DR lives and I gleaned from the context that when he's not in Los

Angeles, he lives somewhere in the Northwest. I learned the location of where he grew up, so I called a friend in that city to fax me the page out of the telephone book with all the listings for DR's surname. There was only one. I called the number and found a friendly relative who kindly gave me a phone number in Los Angeles. Calls to his number in Los Angeles didn't lead to a face-to-face meeting, but were encouraging.

Months later, passing through the Los Angeles airport, I dialed the number again. DR was not in, but, incidentally, he was travelling to my city in a few days, I was told. I should leave my number again and DR would call, came the promise of a friendly secretary and personal assistant. On the way back through Los Angeles three days later, I missed my connecting flight. As the winter fogs were wreaking havoc in the LA skies, I had a few hours of layover in Los Angeles International Airport. I read, tried to smooze my way into the lounge for business class flyers and wandered around the terminal, watching people.

Strolling through the terminal watching individuals in the stream of oncoming crowds close to the gate where I was eventually scheduled to catch my plane home, I saw a man, black suited, turtle-necked, tall, looking GQ suave and aristocratic with blond hair falling professionally over his collar, walking towards me. We made eye contact. He looked vaguely familiar to me. Our eyes locked, but we walked past one another. A few steps past the handsome stranger and suddenly remembering the color photo of the author-artist on the back of the coffee-table book, I realized I had just encountered DR, my long-searched-for artist, actor, writer and thinker. I turned around; he had turned around as well. We came to within six feet of one another.

"Do I know you?" DR asked.

"No," I said, "but you have my name and phone number in your bag. You're DR aren't you?"

"Yes!" he said, "but we haven't met?"

"I've been calling your office for some months now wanting to meet you and talk to you about an art collector friend of mine who would like to see some of your art firsthand, possibly to buy. But no, we've never met before."

"Strange," he mused, "you seem so familiar to me."

"Are you getting on the plane at this gate?" I asked. He nodded. We were scheduled to fly on the same flight.

As we shuffled through the queue boarding the plane, we talked about his art, and I remembered some of the characteristics of his painting with their searching, haunting, spiritual overtones. I was able to ask some fairly informed questions despite my minimal knowledge of art. He chatted about his art and his acting. I explored his spiritual journey, starting with a question about his view of faith versus his view of his ancestor's faith. I referred to a very interesting painting of his called "The Mennonite" that shows a severe character with a head full of cobwebs and a quilt-work of conflicting themes of peace and anger.

"I think I've left that all behind me now," DR said. "That piece 'The Mennonite' is really a caricature of my grandfather. But I think I have really left that far behind me now. I'm in a very different spiritual place at the moment. Though I must admit that the 'Mennonite' keeps appearing in my consciousness, in my dreams, even on the canvas quite often. How do you explain that?"

"Oh, I don't think we leave those strong images of our legacy behind very easily," I volunteered. "They came from beyond us, from a place we had no control

69

over in the first place, so we can't do much about them still being with us, or still imposing themselves on our person, in the second."

We were seated in different sections of the plane, but struck up our conversation again as we moved snail-like through Customs once back on the ground again at our destination. Our conversation continued about his career, his interests and his journey.

"I am still intrigued by the connection between us," DR mused, "there seems to be some kind of karma, some kind of spiritual connection between the two of us the way we met in LA."

"Oh I think it's the Mennonite connection," I suggested, teasingly. His eyes narrowed. I'm not sure he wanted to take me too seriously.

People make a life out of studying the mystical side of their existence because they love that component of their being, with the hope, possibly, of making it more concrete, making it more definable. But the very attractiveness of the mystic quest is its hiddenness, its mystery. We live in such a material world that our mystic side is easily submerged and even denied by so many of the messages of our day. But if we are to be balanced people we need to both acknowledge the mystery there is in and outside of us, and make peace with it.

DR is a person, in my view, who lives mystery; in fact, being mystical and mysterious is part of his self-created image, part of what he wants to present to the world about who and what he is. He markets his mystical side both because he likes that part of himself and also, I would guess, because it protects him from the world, from those who would exploit him. DR's mysterious stance and distance creates awe in others for him and his art; while it draws them to him, it also keeps them away.

Living in a stridently Protestant world most of my waking hours, I sometimes mourn how much our tradition has followed the *zeitgeist* of the world and largely denied the mystery of just plain living, the mystery of faith and the mystery of God. The mystery of God is so richly revealed in symbols, that we don't employ very much, so teasingly delightful in literature, that we don't read much any more, so passionately alive in good poetry, that we don't much study any more, and in the exploring of the Spirit, that we are overly cautious about. For most of us, the dance with the Spirit is too unpredictable, too uncontrollable, too far beyond our comfort zone.

If we're not willing to wonder at our mystical side, if we foolishly, paranoiacally associate it with something dangerous and to be avoided, if we think life is just "about the facts" and not about mystery, we miss so much of God. God is largely mystery—good mystery. He's everyday mystery hanging about the doors of our real and always artificially clear life.

Aunt Anne

They were a gaggle of elderly women who gathered for games every Tuesday morning. While some played shuffleboard on the shiny, waxed and powdered gym floor, the rest of them took to carpet bowling, except for the radical two or three who invaded the male-dominated church-hall pool room. It didn't matter really what games they played, their decades old disputes, arguments and allegiances held strong, and their prejudices and personalities always rose to the surface no matter what. Some of the relatives stuck together because they were relatives; some of them feuded for the same reason.

It was drawn to my attention one Tuesday that there was trouble on the bowling floor, and it was suggested that I go and investigate. The trouble, it seemed, revolved around Aunt Anne and the very disturbing reality that one member of their community group had been found dead in her apartment just two days earlier, and, "She wasn't even one of the sick ones!" I had long ago come to know that the death of one person in a group threatens the rest of the cluster no matter how old or how young the members are, and it was reported that Aunt Anne was not so subtly working her way through her playing partners all the while asking them whether they were ready to die, for after all, "You could be next!"

I headed down to the gym and meandered through the groupings of players, shuffling and chatting, making small talk myself, until I came to the bowlers. Aunt Anne sat in a chair at the end of the bowling carpet. Understandably, the chairs on either side of her were empty. I sat down beside her and leaned my shoulder against hers, being affectionate, being assertive.

"What's up, Aunt Anne? How are you?"

"Not good!" she answered, "not good. People are sure upset about Martha's death. They're so scared!"

"I hear you're not helping!"

"What do you mean, I'm not helping!? Have they come running to you about me again?"

"Well, you know, Aunt Anne, people find it a little disturbing to be told they'll be dying next!"

"I know. But it's true. I might be, you might be. We better be ready!"

Anne wasn't my aunt, but I knew I'd have to get inside her thick self-protective ring if I ever hoped to survive her equally brilliant and devastating verbal torpedoing, those emotional attacks that remind one of a rocket assault. What Aunt Anne called honesty was mostly bluntness and tactlessness. One member of her extended family system said Anne was just missing the relational gene that so many in their clan were without. In any case, I wiggled and endured, and even endeared myself to her, I think, getting past her aggressive defenses and attacks with some warfare of my own, thinking that probably below all that crustiness lived a hungry heart, a deep loneliness and a bushel of regrets, along with a strong need to be accepted, forgiven, loved and cared for.

The furore about who was going to die next faded over a few Tuesdays and life resumed its normal routines on the bowling floor with the news about who was sick, who was hurt, who wasn't talking, who was at the doctors and whose children didn't come home or even phone anymore.

We spend much of our lives looking forward to old age and the time to play without work getting in the way, wintering in the warm South and reading the books we never had time to read when we were younger. But when the "golden years" finally arrive and every year seems shorter, probably because each is a smaller percentage of the whole life we have lived, we need to remind ourselves that being older, being retired and having more free time doesn't diminish our self-worth one iota. We are still just as significant. We still are the only ones who can touch the world in the unique way that we can. The brush God has put in our hand is the only one like it. In wine and in people, age is a value.

Do people present themselves as they are? Is the grouch really a grouch, or does he just want somebody to love him? Does he think he hasn't had enough love in this life yet to warrant a satisfied grin on his face? Does the kind person, on the other hand, smile and reach out because she knows that in presenting herself in pleasantness people will feed back to her the things she needs in order to feel good about herself? Does she accept the responsibility to create a world that is pleasant to her?

As many different faces as there are, so are there as

many ways to face life. Life hands itself out differently to different people, and people respond differently to the same fortunes and misfortunes. Our perceptions are very much determined by our attitudes, by our view of things, by the choices we make in our analysis and diagnosis of things.

God wants the best for us, every day. If we attach ourselves to his coattails, if we pin our soul fortunes to Jesus, who is the gate to the God field, God doesn't necessarily throw material things our way. In fact things may get worse in the material, and even in the social sense because the rain falls on the good and the bad, the believer and the unbeliever. Much of what happens to us in life is random, but what is not random nor accidental is that God can start a transformation in our attitudes in response to all of life, and in so doing we gain a more positive way to filter everything that happens to us. That's how the God of Abraham, Jacob and Isaac, that old God of the Bible who has been around forever, can impact us every day.

The Revolutionary, The Outlaw & The *Babushka*

How she shook off her strong pacifist and pietistic roots and became a fringe member of the urban-terrorist Baader-Meinhof group, I never really found out. But we became friends in spite of my apolitical leanings and she introduced me to her political friends. Friends who in their intellectually sophisticated, multisyllabic German loved to talk about *socialismus*, Berlin, the East Bloc, the Russian Experiment, American Imperialism, and Angela Davis and the Black Panthers. They described the Marxist realities they believed must be applied to the German political landscape and beyond, if there was ever going to be truth and justice in their world's future. One day I heard them scheming about springing a friend out of a Berlin jail and whisking him to a hoped-for socialist heaven in Cuba. I shook my head.

Her friends were well-off, middle class students and professionals who were politically passionate—some in a quiet, intellectual way, some in a fist-waving way—not so unlike many Germans before them. I, on the other hand, was a long-haired, garishly dressed and sandalled, politically naive Canadian—a good time Charlie, passionate in a laid-back sort of way, mostly about finding out who I was outside of and far away from my own tight, pietistic, Anabaptist first-generation Canadian community.

I laughed at my new German friends' politics; they thought I was joking. Somehow, in spite of my irreverence, they folded me into the edges of their circle of intellectual Marxists and would-be social democratic political reformers. We spent weekends together discussing issues, eating rich foods and drinking the necessary Rhine wines. On one of these weekend retreats an informal suggestion was made, and then a few days later a further invitation arrived in the mail asking me to accompany my new friends to Moscow. It was 1970; the Cold War was still icy. I accepted. Why not? It sounded like adventure, intrigue, even some education. I had listened to enough of my Dad's stories to know that Russia was the place of my ancestral, spiritual, geographical and political roots, and at my age that was beginning to take on some interest for me.

Ten days later we boarded a train in the student city of Karlsruhe, to ride to Berlin to marvel at the simple wonder of Communist East Berlin, and to walk its barren streets. I thought it quite dull and deprived actually; my German friends, however, thought it honest and beautiful in its bleakness, and romantic even. It was enchanting like a stark desert is, they said, a healthy hush in a noisy world going crazy.

For some days we wandered the streets of both East and West Berlin, noting the differences between the two German-speaking cities. East Berlin had few cars and no neon lights, its only colorful distractions the huge posters of Lenin and Marx glowering down on the hurried populace. It exuded no socialistic *joi de vive* or the jauntiness of freedom. It felt permanently hushed. Or was I too propagandized by another system?

West Berlin, on the other hand, was loud and raucous, garish and gaudy, materialistic, even vulgar and unabashedly immoral. This city of the west was never silent.

Berlin touched a strange chord in my being, especially in light of my commitment at that time to test all the edges of my life. I longed for a spiritual shower after a day on its streets. I was surprised by these feelings I thought I had forgotten, of needing a soul bath, the remembered childhood guilt after sneaking behind bushes to smoke dried ragweed stalks with my cousins, or skipping afternoon church services and recklessly trying aloud every swear word we had ever heard.

After a few days of tasting, touching, smelling and feeling Berlin, and after all the mingling of the West versus East and East versus West rhetoric, and people trying to convince me which side was actually freer, West Berlin or East Berlin, with good arguments on both sides, we finally climbed aboard an Aeroflot flight to Moscow. I began to wonder what I had gotten myself into. I hadn't asked a lot of questions what this was all about. I told the young German sitting beside me that I wondered what I was doing. He, whose goal in life seemed becoming more American than most Americans would want to be, responded, "This is a happening, man. Just let it experience!" in a thick German accent that sounded far from the melting pots of New York, South Carolina or Los Angeles.

The Russian sweets served to the passengers were virtually inedible and the airliner free fell through the air at one point—reminding me I had religious roots that probably needed to be re-explored again. It's interesting how religious we get when death seems near or even when we're at thirty thousand feet.

Who actually underwrote the trip, I never knew, and in that Cold War era, I was probably wise not to have asked. I know it cost me nearly nothing. We landed in Moscow. I remember my passport disappearing as my protest to an armed customs officer with what I thought were tough sounding words about the Geneva Convention fell on deaf and cynical ears.

I remember the huge, grotesque monument outside Moscow honoring the millions of Russians killed in war—my history studies had never alerted me to the staggering losses the Russians had suffered. We checked into the Intourist Hotel, a shabby place by any standards, with one washroom per floor, the kind one should stay in only so long as one can hold one's breath. I checked my room for listening devices, though I probably wouldn't have recognized one if I found it. We had our first of many Russian dinners of liver and rice, washed down with sour soda water. We started to fan out around the city of Moscow. Were we watched and followed? I doubt it. And if we were, not for long. One glance at me on a Moscow street would convince any politico I was harmless and maybe even less. We hailed a taxicab and drove through miles of Moscow streets. Dropping us off at Red Square, the driver cancelled the fare when one of my political friends in the back seat gave him a *Playboy* magazine.

We gazed in awe at the Square, taking in Lenin's Tomb against the Wall and the poignant spires of St. Basil's, and we joined the Moscow bustle in the Gum department store. One could feel history in the air of Red Square or was it the voices of all the people who had lived and died there?

The Gum department store of 1971, though magnificent by Russian standards, was most notable to this North American and his German friends by its starkness and the utter scarcity of consumer goods and products. For little money we bought a few items as souvenirs. We left the store and wandered the streets, sometimes aware of soldiers and policemen eyeing us, but at other times able to walk quite freely around the parks, the public markets, even the black market streets of the Opera area and the bridges across the wide expanses of the Moskva River. We decided that Lenin's tomb would be visited later, already knowing that as foreign tourists we would be whisked to the front of the patient Russian six-hour queue to see the "Father of Russia" lying in state, unspoiled like a psalmic messiah.

I went for a stroll towards a bridge across the wide Moskva River near the Opera house. A young man, several years my senior, sidled up beside me and asked, "What time is it?" I pulled my pocket watch tethered by a retired bootlace from my jean pocket and stated the time.

"Ah, you are Canadian. I know from your accent! It is a very good country that you come from." He smiled, clearly attempting a patriotic buttering-up to gain some kind of advantage or favor. "Let's walk!" he pointed, "over the bridge, where no one can listen to us." We started a slow stroll onto the bridge. "Where are you from in Canada?" His well-articulated English sounded like he might have graced the halls of Oxford. "Is it true that there is unemployment in Canada?" he asked. I sensed his question had little to do with wanting an answer.

"Yes!" I said, studying his face in sidelong glances, trying to discern whether he was an economic opportunist or a dangerous character with intentions I couldn't even imagine.

"Hmm," he answered, "I guess our government doesn't lie to us all the time." I guessed that meant something profound but I didn't quite know what. He shifted, apparently feeling safe and proceeded. "Do you have anything to sell me?"

"Like what?" I asked, a little surprised.

"Your blue jeans. Your suede boots. Some pens. Ladies' nylons. A Playboy magazine! Whatever you like. I buy things from tourists I can't buy in our stores."

"What's your point?" I ventured, suddenly feeling like an amateur journalist probing for deeper truths behind what was happening. "You're playing the black market here. Why?"

My Russian friend, blond and blue-eyed, looked back over his shoulder like a hunted dealer, his actions pseudo-serious and overly dramatic. I almost expected him to open his jacket and show me the wares lining it, but he said, "You know we can protest nothing in this society. Words and demonstrations get us arrested and jailed. Working the black market is tolerated, to a point, and though I can say nothing, by my well-known activity on the market the officials know that I protest. This is all a political protest. I would prefer to live in New York or Los Angeles and be free!"

"Angela Davis wouldn't think that you'd be free in New York or LA!" I thought, but remained quiet. I didn't really think his words were about freedom anyway. They seemed too calculated, too rehearsed.

The blue jeans and suede boots I wore were the only trousers and shoes I owned; they could not be sold or given away, they could only be forcefully torn off and stolen, I told my new acquaintance. Why I would suggest such an idea completely escaped my good sense as I recalled that conversation later, as I quickly confessed that I wasn't wearing any ladies' nylons and had neither pens nor *Playboy* magazines. Whether I, at that point, was seen as a zero prospect, economically, politically or otherwise, I don't know, but my well-rehearsed Russian friend suddenly remembered an earlier appointment across the bridge, shook my hand and left me to wander back to my hotel on my own.

Two hours later I was at the front of the long queue waiting to see the remains of Vladimir Illich Lenin lying in state in a mausoleum outside the Kremlin Wall, as it had faithfully done since his death in 1924. I stood in the doorway of the mausoleum between two very serious Russian soldiers, waiting to be allowed into the sacred sanctum of the Russian saint. Finally the signal came and a group of us shuffled down the flights of stairs into the chamber below Red Square that housed Lenin's coffin, his body in full view under a clear Plexiglas dome. The figure looked familiar, like someone in Madame Tussaud's Wax Museum. I remembered the elderly Russian woman outside who had told me, through a young interpreter, that Lenin's body had mysteriously not decomposed after death like it says in the Bible, and hence we could know he was of sacred importance. As we moved in a perfect U around the bier, we dared not speak, none of us, for Russian and tourist were required to exhibit an awful respect for Lenin. The eight or ten soldiers standing ready with bayoneted rifles alongside the shuffling line studied us sternly for indications of disrespect or evil intentions, I guess, of wanting to harm the poor man already forty-some years dead. I found out later somebody had once tried to bomb the body. In any case, I was wearing a military-like jacket with large pockets. Suddenly one of the guards lowered his rifle and, pointing the barrel dangerously toward me, stuck the bayonet on his weapon between my arm and my body and lifted my arm away from my side. With a free hand he then felt the bulge in my pocket to see whether or not its contents, a cheap ladies' scarf bought earlier at the Gum store, might be an incendiary threat to Vlladimir and his guards. Dying a hundred deaths myself with this sudden aggressive action toward me, I immediately lost my interest in contemplating the waxy, historical face of Lenin who had sent my forefathers scurrying from Russia to Canada decades ago. My heart beating wildly, I impatiently shuffled my way out of that macabre mausoleum into the relatively free and cool air of Red Square not far from where Stalin's remains were still buried in the Wall of the Kremlin. Like my German travel mates, I was acquiring a certain feeling about socialism and communism though not exactly in a parallel fashion; my political being was being awakened.

The next day I stayed on the streets of Moscow and avoided the tourist spots of dead Russian leaders and soldiers. Everywhere I went Russian children pressed little pins of Russian bears and red Lenins into my hand and tried their school-learned English on me. Discovering I was Canadian, virtually all of them launched into assertions that Russians were better hockey players than Canadians were. How I wished I could have seen then into a Paul Henderson future, but I just hope they remembered my feigned outrage that they could even contemplate that Russian hockey players were superior to Canadians.

Before long I was sitting on a low stone wall in front of an upscale hotel, a hotel for foreigners only, which housed shops at which only foreigners could buy a wide array of foreign products no Russian would ever see, unless he had the courage and cash to engage a shrewd black marketeer. I must have been an odd sight to the Russian passersby with my bright red and white T-shirt, blue jeans and bare feet. I had kicked off my sandals. My unkempt, shoulder length hair seemed to attract a more boisterous crowd than waited

to see Lenin's body, and soon I was the gazed-upon
spectacle of an ever-increasing crowd of snorting and
crowing Russians, most of them elderly women with
print dresses, kerchiefs, brown stockings rolled above
heavy and broken-down shoes and plastic mesh shop-
ping bags. One woman, leathery-faced and nearly
toothless, except for long incisors, reached out and
touched my shoulder to see if I was real perhaps. Her
laugh cackling like a Shakespearean witch escaped
from Macbeth contradicted her eyes, bright and dancing and I sensed some charm about her. Apparently
she thought me at least amusing, if not ridiculous. A
boy of about ten years moved into place, standing side-
ways between me and the woman, volunteering by his
actions to be the language courier between us.

"Where are you from?" shouted the woman, as the
boy translated in a decent schoolboy English.

"From Canada!" I answered, grinning, enjoying the
attention of a growing crowd. The old peasant woman, the *babushka*, shrugged her shoulders. She had
never heard of Canada.

"Why aren't you wearing any shoes?"

"I don't want to wear shoes!" I answered. The
babushka and her cronies guffawed at the absurdity of
not wanting to wear shoes. I guessed they had lived
most of their lives either without shoes or had endured bad shoes.

"Does your mother know you are here?" she continued, her friends nodding their agreement at the question.

"Yes!"

"Why is it that she lets you travel all the way to Russia, but she doesn't make you cut your hair so you
don't look like a girl?" The crowd howled.

I never answered. By this time a policeman had
pushed his way through the zoo-like crowd of gawkers

and shouted at me, the monkey, to move on. I slipped into my sandals and walked away.

It has often been said that we become the people we spend time with. I have often wondered about these encounters of mine with a revolutionary, an outlaw and a *babushka*, how much I was meeting myself, how much I was exploring the idea of what I was by any definition of those nomenclatures.

There's a delightful little Yiddish story idea called a *tisch mit menschen* (a table of people) which describes in old European Jewish terms virtually every kind of character and personality type known to their community, and really any human community anywhere in the world. Some time after I had written this piece, I recalled that old Yiddish idea and thought of how interesting and how wonderful a conversation between a revolutionary, an outlaw and a *babushka* might be if they could get around a table at the same time.

What would be said if each one of these three could stop aggressively creating their own worlds and enter into a real conversation, the kind that means at least as much listening as talking. A revolutionary inclined to throw bombs, who carries a political chip on her shoulder, an outlaw trying to beat "the system," and the *babushka*, disdainful of anything unfamiliar, carry one thing in common—anger. That they could compare and contrast what anger is with great insight and with great interchange goes without saying.

I don't know what gave all three their anger, but I would guess that a sense of injustice is what drove all of them. God, as found in Scripture, is really a God of justice. No matter how revolutionary our thoughts and actions, no matter how criminal we may have become, no matter how much hurt has cut us down, the Creator, Savior God of the Universe who seeks the best for his created beings every day can remake angry souls into joyous laughers and can equip them to become dancers in the streets of forever, even now, even today, should they ask.

The BMW Driver

Whenever the boss said, "Take a week off!" (and he said it quite often), I would roll up my sleeping bag, fill up my green and gray knapsack with life's travelling necessities and walk out the long winding driveway to the road. From there I could see the road in both directions, snaking its way around hillocks, through wood lots, dropping into and rising up out of little German villages. To me the scenery was calendar-like all year round. From there I could see a car approaching from either direction at least one or two kilometers before it came to where I was standing, waiting for an adventure.

One early cloudy morning I stood out on the road, smelling the apples that had fallen off the trees lining the road and been smashed on the pavement by the tires of the passing cars, and wondered what I would eat that day, where I would lay my head that night. The not knowing stirred some excitement within me. I heard the hum of a car coming from the east so I stayed on the north side of the road that would set me travelling in the same direction as the car. The driver slowed his automobile, curious to see a hitchhiker way out here in the country, and stopped and kindly picked me up.

The German farmer steering his work-a-day gray Opel through the hills of southern Germany had little understanding for a Canadian losing his teen years just "touring" Europe, but he had enough of a heart to give me a ride. I resisted the temptation to argue with him as he shot out various opinions, his voice having that edge to it that has always invited me to disputation.

My driver dropped me off just outside Sinsheim. I walked down to one of the Autobahn entries and waited. It appeared that I was heading west and north this day. That's the only way this road led.

A huge blue truck with bright red rims groaned to a stop just a little past me. I ran to the truck and pulled myself part way up the ladder. The driver impatiently beckoned me in. I sighed the hitchhiker's success-sigh and threw my bedroll up through the high open door of the truck. It was more spotless than it could have been the moment it came out of the factory. My eyes at seat level as I was clambering up the ladder, I saw my sleeping bag bounce against the twelve-inch thick feather blanket and its huge pillow spread out immaculately just behind the driver and passenger seats. The driver growled at me to be careful and I suspect he nearly changed his mind about having me along in his truck. Nevertheless, I chorused a good southern German "Excuse me please!" and pulled myself up into the sparkling truck cab. By the time I had found a place around my feet for my knapsack and bedroll, I was wishing I had had my hiking boots shined or at least checked them for grass and dirt flecks before getting into this pristine tractor, but Mr. Clean was already making his way through his truck's gears towards highway speed.

Our conversation was a little stiff; he only spoke a German dialect. I hardly spoke German anything. We managed, however, and I soon discerned he was only going to Heidelberg. I told him I was going further, I'd already been in Heidelberg. My jump down from the semi-truck on the side of the Autobahn a half hour later left me in a bad and illegal place to get a ride, so I hitched up my shoulders under the straps of my knapsack, tightened the waist belt and started trudging down the shoulder of the road.

The Autobahn traffic howled and hissed past me. Mercedes and BMW's flashing their headlights in the fast lanes warned other motorists ahead of them travelling at less than 180 kilometers per hour to please move over. I heard a car gearing down as I walked along, my back to the oncoming traffic. A burgundy BMW, shiny, new, sleek, sophisticated and looking like it dared anyone to just try driving it slowly, swerved and skidded onto the shoulder in front of me, its brake lights bright, its tires nearly smoking, as the driver reigned in his rubber tired rocket. He punched his mechanical stallion into reverse, back to where I was walking. I had never ridden in a BMW before. This would be good. And fast, I thought.

"Get in!" shouted the driver, pushing open the passenger door, his slightly German accented English twinged with something Oxfordian.

"Thank you!"

"Where are you going?" he asked, warmly.

"As far as I can!"

"Where are you from?"

"I'm Canadian!"

"Oh, that's good. Welcome to Germany. Your impressive Prime Minister, Pierre Trudeau, shuffled his cabinet yesterday. What do you think of the new appointments?" The driver's right hand rested on the gearshift, his knuckles showing up through the stitched openings in a leather driving glove, his other hand steered the car. The needle on the speedometer touched 190 as we careened along this eight-lane highway extravaganza.

"Cabinet shuffle!" I snorted. "Who cares?"

The driver dropped his foot off the accelerator and veered the car toward the extreme right lane of the Autobahn, stopping nearly as quickly, I think, as he had when he first saw me on the road a few minutes earlier.

"Who cares? Who cares?" he shouted. "You are a Canadian and you say, 'Who cares?' about a cabinet shuffle in your own country. You don't deserve to be travelling Europe. You can't learn anything here if you know and care so little about your own country. Get out! Get out!"

I was glad the car had stopped by the time he finished his speech, so that I didn't have to get out on the move. I was back on the shoulder of the road in a bad place again almost before I knew it.

An unusually friendly highway patrolman wearing a white helmet and a green leather jacket to match his green Mercedes with its white door offered me a lift to the better spot on the road for other rides, for more lessons.

Later that evening I walked into the Frankfurt train station. I found a news kiosk and bought the international Newsweek magazine with its one-page report on Canada. I found out who our new cabinet ministers were. I was interested for the first time. I may still know who they were.

How do we learn? With all the teachers in the world and all the research being done to understand the art of pedagogy, we still don't really know how people learn. We know each person learns differently than others, but we haven't been able to unlock the secret of learning, yet.

I have come to know, however, that we learn best what we discover ourselves. I had never bothered to pay attention to who our cabinet ministers might be. I had never been motivated to know even the slightest of the intricacies of our governmental system. I had never discerned that such might be important. When an assertive foreigner shamed me, and shame doesn't always work nor would I recommend it as a positive teaching method, I discovered how to find out who Canadian cabinet ministers are, and how interesting previously uninteresting things can suddenly become. I take an interest in the existence of cabinet ministers today because I made the discovery that cabinet ministers are important at some level to our living. The only thing the BMW driver did was throw me the key to learn what I found I wanted to learn.

I think, too, that God holds keys and drops them in conspicuous places and sometimes right on our heads. Nevertheless, we learn things when we are motivated to learn them. When it becomes very clear to us that there is a good reason to know something, we learn it. And God is a creative and caring BMW driver zooming along our life's road finding ways to encourage us to learn what we need to learn.

The Burglars

I don't know where Mom and Dad had gone with my uncle and aunt, but they were gone for the night leaving the nine or ten of us kids at home without adult supervision. We played around in the yard in the dying light of dusk waiting for nightfall to begin our Hide 'n Seek game, a game wonderfully enhanced by the darkness of night. We waited around the hydro pole—the yard light—in the middle of the barnyard. This post was the safe "home base" and center of the game.

Just before dark, an old beat-up pickup truck pulled into the yard. We kids crowded around it. We knew every vehicle and its owners within a ten-mile radius of the farm, but we didn't know this truck nor who its passengers were. A somewhat wizened old man and his two elderly, wrinkled, weathered-looking female passengers took up the whole of the truck seat. The woman against the passenger door rolled down her window with some difficulty and with a cracking voice asked if she might have a drink of water.

One of my sisters ran into the house and scooped a

plastic cup full of water from the water pail. She
brought it to the window of the truck and handed it
to the woman, who took it in her shaky hands and
slowly raised it to her lips. Some of us remembered
later that the driver was busy looking around the yard
and seemed not at all interested in this gaggle of kids
around his truck who were more than interested in
him. The woman nursed her water for a few seconds,
drank almost nothing, and then said, "Thank You!"
The driver started up his truck and wheeled it around
and down the driveway that was treed on one side, but
open to the wide prairie on the other. We resumed
our play.

The Hide 'n Seek game wore us out and ended itself when one of the big boys tore open his forehead
while trying to run underneath a crossbeam under the
combine in the dark. We wondered whether he needed a doctor. Instead of calling one, we all just ate
some huge bowls of cornflakes and got ready for bed.
The big girls all over the bed in Mom and Dad's room,
the little kids in the girls' room and the two big boys,
my brother and cousin John, in Jake's room. The window in Jake's room was wide open and years later I understood why his window was almost always open at
night. It opened onto the roof of the porch from
which one could easily get down to the ground.

We went to bed late. We always did when the
cousins were over because of all the talking and laughing. We remembered how the year before we had been
visiting them on their dairy farm two days drive and
more away, and how we had made a bet with their
neighbors' teenagers that our cows would give more
milk than theirs the next morning. We laughed how
we had simply skipped milking our cows that night
knowing that the next morning their engorged udders
would break all production records and leave their

neighbor's cows looking like no counts in the milk production department. What the poor cows would be producing a few days later we didn't worry about, and we certainly hoped our fathers would never find out. But we won the bet. Nevertheless, we all went to sleep eventually this night remembering the adventures we had had.

A few hours later, my brother was awakened by the sound of a motor purring. It sounded like a car or a small truck. Hearing the motor first idle and then stop running altogether, he slipped out of bed and bent out through the wide-open window of his room that looked out over the roof of the porch, out over the garden and beyond that to the road that ran past our place.

It was one of those nights with a clear sky, bright diamond stars and a large moon that lit up the countryside in a beautiful deep dark purple hue, that was bright enough to cast shadows, and bright enough, too, for daring teenagers to drive Dad's car on the country roads without the lights on.

In the bright moonlight, then, my brother saw that same old truck with its three passengers who had come searching for water earlier in the evening. It was now parked out on the road. Moonlight reflected off its side windows.

My brother leaned even further out his window. Now he could see the pick-up's driver slowly walking up the lane, passing in and out of the shadows the trees cast across the driveway. Every few steps the driver would stop. Probably he was listening for sounds that would warn him he was being found out, or for fear that a territorial farm dog would suddenly come growling out of the nighttime shadows and botch the whole operation. My brother noted the intruder would stand for quite a few moments each time he

94

stopped, not in any hurry, it seemed, to finish his mission, whatever it was.

My brother slipped on his trousers and tiptoed out of his room, down the curved and linoleum-covered stairs to the kitchen and out into the porch. He felt around in the dark behind the door for Dad's old 38-55 Winchester rifle, a rifle that would have made any western cowboy proud, with its long hexagon barrel and easy lever action. Feeling up on the top shelf of the cupboard where the shells for the "big" gun and the 22 shells were, his hand easily picked up a 38 shell. He slid it into the opening on the side of the rifle and cocked the lever. The shell was now in the chamber. He slipped back into the kitchen. He could easily make his way around the table and the chairs by the moonlight streaming in the large windows of the house, and stepped out the back door facing away from the driveway, making sure the screen door wouldn't slam. Moving around the outside of the house, he poked his head around the corner to see if the intruder was still on the lane. Sure enough, there he was, some fifty feet closer to the house than my brother had last seen him from the bedroom window, but still some distance down the lane. Tiptoeing now in the dewy grass, carefully like a cat, my brother made his way in the shadows away from the house toward the road, keeping the row of trees between himself and the visitor, who must have sensed or heard something, for he hadn't moved in quite a few moments. My brother moved past the man, some seventy feet or so west of him and kept stealthily moving further north of him. My brother then cut east through the row of trees, still carefully silent, until he stood on the driveway between the night visitor and his truck, waiting on the road, with its two passengers probably wondering what was taking so long. By this time, the in-

95

truder must have felt safe to move ahead, for he moved another thirty feet closer to the house. My brother stood in a shadow but could easily see the walker in the moonlight, quite close to the house now but still on the driveway. It was time for the play.

Now it must be said that Dad's 38-55 was an old gun, a slow gun, its ammunition clumsy and heavy, hence needing a good load of gunpowder to make it effective. And therefore a loud gun. An excessively loud gun. My brother knew that and that's what his plan was all about. Raising the stock of the nearly antique gun to his shoulder and pointing its barrel at a 45-degree angle to the ground and pointing at some stars high above the southern prairie horizon, high above the head of the intruder who was standing still again, my brother pulled the trigger. A red-orange tongue of flame shot out the end of the gun barrel like a dragon's belch and the sound that echoed off the trees and ricocheted off the house, the barn and the sheds and rolled across the prairie fields that night seemed louder than a ten-megaton bomb with a summer thunderclap added on.

Every one of us in the house was awake before the sound explosion had half died down. The poor visitor must have nearly joined the cow in the cat-and-the-fiddle story, and when his feet hit the ground they were heading for his truck at a speed that the old truck itself could probably never reach and would make any Olympian proud. He obviously had no idea from which direction the sound had come, for he ran straight down the lane toward my brother and passed him within a foot-and-a-half, but never saw him. Terms like "his heart was in his mouth", or "he had the bit in his mouth" could have been applied to the scurrying visitor, for he tore off the lane, round the graveled corner and up to his truck, jumped in, found the keys in the ignition, started it, popped the clutch, stalled the beast, started it again, and spun gravel swerving to get away as fast as he could down the road and away from this dangerous farmyard.

We never saw the truck or its occupants again. My dad was not impressed when he found out the next day that a gun was used to scare away potential robbers, but we kids, a brother, some sisters and the cousins, sure thought my brother was the bravest, most creative scare-guy we had ever heard of, and we started to invent how we might have been part of this brave escapade.

Time often changes our view of things and my brother's protective, defensive vigilantism and his wild-west one-man posse antics wouldn't seem so innocent and creative today. To stop someone from doing something dastardly is already far enough and away from "turning the other cheek", to say nothing of hatching a clever plan to stop an intruder and scare him silly at the same time with a high-powered rifle in the dark at some great risk to everyone, is another.

What this vignette is about is the creativity and the courage of a big brother taking seriously an old-fashioned responsibility for all the younger kids in the house. On the other hand, it is about using fear and surprise to turn what might have been an intruder's violent intention into a delightful story of "the bad guy" himself running in terror. Instead of him visiting fear and dread on others, fear and dread chased him over the dark horizon in the fastest possible way. It is the big bad wolf getting caught in Grandma's bedclothes before he can harm the child.

Fear and courage and creativity are the stuff of life.

They flow in and out of everyone's life with some regularity. We know all three of these things in our daily lives. To be creative in each of our own unique ways is common; we are created in the image of the Creator. And to know fear which chills us is also everydayish. But courage takes more. Courage doesn't usually just happen, it needs to be grasped and thrown, or run with.

It is not an accident that God says, "Fear not, be of great courage. . ." for those very words are needed by everyone of us on occasion. That God has given us the creativity to respond is a double miracle. God knows that somewhere every day fear and courage are part of human living. That's why his creativity, which we can exercise, is more available than a fire extinguisher too often too far away from the emergency. God knows that courage and creativity may be needed any second, that is why his "breath" and his "power" are on standby always, everywhere.

Mr. Huma

M r. Huma had a full head of hair, high up on his head like a Bert and Ernie doll, but it was thinning and shorn around his ears. His sideburns were fashionably long and his nose and ear hairs were mature and well established. Mr. Huma wore the same dreary, dark suit almost every day and the knees and the seat of his trousers were shiny to match the elbows of his jacket.

I think Mr. Huma liked kids and cared about them, but the educational system had somehow put a permanent ban on teachers showing they liked kids, I guess, for fear any affection would corrupt students who felt affirmed. Mr. Huma taught Math, Grade 9 Math, with its geometry, theorems and algebra, and he felt a deep sense of call to drive the stuff into the heads of his students.

Mr. Huma was somewhat deaf, however, and his hearing aids hardly compensated for what had become lost to him. Eccentric and too old and too tired to care to keep abreast of high school student antics anymore, he drifted into a kind of pedagogical oblivion though still in the center of all the classroom action and his desire to teach the math facts of life.

Mr. Huma loved tests, at least he loved administering tests. And he had a keen sense of making sure no one could ever cheat on a test. As he handed out the test papers, he would shout out the rules of testing integrity, sometimes adding his own twist: "Anyone caught smiling or laughing during the test will be deemed to be cheating and will receive an automatic 0%."

One day early in the school year Mr. Huma had everyone in the class settled, papered and pencil-readied for a test. Mr. Huma announced, "Begin!" like a starter pistol and trotted out of the room, leaving the door open and us to our honor as to whether we could cheat or not. Or so we thought. Some fifteen seconds or so after his departure, those of us who were not too deeply engrossed in the writing of our test yet could see the very tops of Mr. Huma's hair inching into view around the edge of the doorframe at floor level. Slowly, slowly, more and more of his head came into view until all of his hair, his long forehead and one eye could be seen coming into view like a slow ship slipping into harbor from around an island, his cheek pressed to the floor. Mr. Huma had lain himself down in the hallway outside the room and was checking that no one was cheating on his "life-changing" test. To not laugh at this peculiar man lying on the floor, was more difficult than scoring 100% in Grade 9 Math, and more than one of his students reported a 0% for having snorted and burst out laughing at the ridiculous spectacle of this teacher who took his teaching task seriously beyond the sensible.

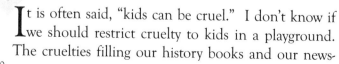

It is often said, "kids can be cruel." I don't know if we should restrict cruelty to kids in a playground. The cruelties filling our history books and our newspapers are seldom the work of children, but are the work of adults, volitional adults, who take it upon themselves to see their victims as not worth the dignity of being treated with respect, let alone awe. We humans, too often, make those who are different from ourselves less than worthy of dignity, and once we have made short shrift of their dignity, reduced them to a lesser being, we can do anything dastardly to them that we can imagine.

It takes a mature and open person to see the eccentric person as a gift, as a delight. Mr. Huma was eccentric, but we students actually felt a great deal of affection for him, though we also thought him a little silly. But seeing someone as silly doesn't need to lead to ostracizing or demeaning that person. Seeing someone as silly can even mean we try to protect him or at least cut him some slack and give him some way for his unique expression of life.

Mr. Huma lying on the floor and checking to see whether we would cheat or not, really was a teacher who had our best interests at heart. It didn't seem to matter to him, nor did he even notice that we thought his antics humorous. What mattered to him were our grades, whether we knew our math and whether we walked with integrity in our math class. It all, obviously, mattered more than whether his suit stayed clean or not.

We don't have to agree with someone, nor do we have to have everyone made up in our image to be acceptable. God created enough unique beings to fill the world and no two are identical. What is identical is that he loves each one of us, each with our own unique warts and hairs and beauty. One can walk out every day knowing that today's journey is not outside the ability of God to love us.

Grandma Tripp

I was three or four years old when I first met Grandma Tripp. She lived with her son Robert, his wife Edith, and their nine kids in a house that almost no one in the world would say was big enough for twelve people. But it was never considered that Grandma should be living somewhere else. Grandma helped around the house, she was another mom as it were, an appreciated "taken for granted" caregiver who lent stability, compassion and discipline to the Tripp household.

I don't know why we were at the Tripp's the day in question, but we, my mom and I, were there. The Tripp kitchen uniquely blended the smells of cigarette smoke, barn odors and food cooking on the wood stove. The usual gaggle of Tripp kids must have been away because I remember becoming intrigued by what this wonderfully friendly little old lady with the white hair, the longish dress and the little furry slippers was doing. She was sitting in a high-backed rocking chair with a basket of different colored string balls at her feet whose single strands led up to her lap, where her

hands and the two long needles in them worked back
and forth like the pumping machine I always watched
and heard in the grain elevator.

"What are you doing?" I asked.

"I'm knitting." Grandma Tripp answered.

"What's that?"

"It's making things like mittens out of balls of
string," she smiled. "I make all of my grandchildren
mittens every year."

"Will you make me mittens?" I asked. "My mom
doesn't know how to knit." Grandma Tripp smiled
and glanced at my mother, but said nothing.

On my next birthday some months later, Robert
dropped off a soft package wrapped in tissue paper for
me. A little card fell out of the package as I tore the
paper off, and Mom said, "You got a birthday present
from Grandma Tripp. She's knitted you some mittens."

Every year on my birthday, in a size slightly bigger
and in colors different than last year's, until my 18th
birthday, Grandma Tripp made sure I got the mittens
she had knitted me for the next year. I wonder if I
ever told her how much they meant to me. Grandma
Tripp died a long time ago. The warmth of her giving
is still here.

W hy some people have the resources to be kind
while others persist in cruelty and meanness
can be partially explained by circumstances, history,
psychology, personality, character and family system
patterns, but not completely. Kindness is a gift that
some people share so easily, and in so doing they
warm up people's hearts, families, space and time.
Forty-something years after Grandma Tripp started

knitting me mitts I am still overwhelmed by the memory of a busy grandmother, with more than enough mitts to knit every year, knitting another pair for someone who would pull them on and run out into the snow probably without even thinking of saying "Thank you!"

God gave us more than mitts: he gave us his son, and meaning, purpose and undreamed-of personal fulfillment. When Grandma Tripp gave me mitts, she touched forever in my psyche the awe of receiving something wonderful. Grandma Tripp introduced me to the experience of being at the receiving end of a giving God being kind every day.

Mrs. Bulton

I was too young to have ever been in Mrs. Bulton's class, but the stories my older siblings and my cousins brought home about her were so remarkable it feels like I was there. I can see the events that made her infamous in our little one-room school community; I heard the accounts so often.

I see Jack Davidson, a lumbering, big kid so unenamoured with school he probably should not have bothered being there, even the few times he came, doing the forbidden—taking a drink of water from the school water pail without Mrs. Bulton's permission. I can still see Mrs. Bulton hurling herself across the room, her long legs covering the oiled floor in a second, in her hand the most feared and ultimate teacher's weapon, the wooden yardstick.

I don't think Jack was a bad kid in school—he wouldn't have bothered to expend the energy it takes to aggravate a teacher and he was too good-natured to tease the younger kids, but he was also too adult to think he would have to ask someone for a drink of water that was within easy reach. Besides that, he was the one who had walked to the Taylor farm a quarter mile away at recess to get that water from their well. So he just heaved himself up out of his ridiculous desk, went over to the table where the water pail stood and dipped himself some water in the white metal dipper with its red rim and red handle and drank no differently than he would at home.

The younger kids all thought that Jack was funny, no matter what he did. They howled in delight as he tried to saddle up the little painted pony he rode to school and tied up in the school barn. Whenever he threw the saddle on the little horse, it grabbed the wooden plank of its hay-manger in its long brown teeth and sucked air into its belly with a weird backwards sucking sound until the horse looked like a balloon with head, feet and a tail ready to rise into the air. As Jack swore at his horse, he would lean back and plant a kick into the belly of the pony that almost lifted it off its feet, but somehow, in spite of the kicks, the pony would retain too much air in it's belly for Jack to tighten the cinch of the saddle properly. After a few more kicks and huge hilarious grunts from the horse, Jack would get the saddle somewhat tightened. Leading the horse out of the barn he would swing onto it, invariably leaving his school bag on the barn floor. The horse would start, without any urging from Jack, toward home. Out past the schoolhouse, past the flagpole, out the gate and right around the corner post of the fence it walked, head down. But then, just as it passed the corner, the pony would let its stomach of air out with a gush, the saddle cinch would go slack, suddenly inches far too long, the saddle would slip to the side and Jack would get dumped onto the ground. The horse would stop. Jack would swear, as much for the benefit of the audience waiting and watching for this drama, get up out of the ditch, kick the horse once more as if this was a necessary ritual. The horse would quietly stand while Jack repositioned the saddle, its cinch secure this time around the flattened belly of the horse. The kids laughed and waved. Jack grinned, and if he felt like it, he might be in school again in a few days.

Jack wasn't bad; he was cool and unexcitable actually, far too good-natured to be any trouble to anyone, even his horse did its little routine just to make sure the boy knew who was in charge. The horse was really a good little animal friend and Jack seemed to love the beast. If Mrs. Bulton, or any of the other teachers who passed through this one-room school on their Letters of Permit, would have only let him, his proficient drawings of that horse and other animals would have given him a sense of some success at school beyond anything he ever experienced doing math drills, diagramming sentences, being the first one out of the spelling bee, or memorizing Latin roots.

But to have to ask a teacher for a drink of water that he himself had carried a quarter of a mile trying not to spill on the way was too much for Jack. So he drank and Mrs. Bulton came at him with her yardstick like a Vandal swordsman. Jack kept drinking as she came toward him. As the first blow from her wicked stick was about to strike him across the head or on his shoulder, Jack would grab the weapon end of the stick. Calmly he would keep drinking. Mrs. Bulton gyrated on the other end of the yardstick, for the wildly threatening and free end had just become disabled in the strong hand of a big farm boy whose stubbornness suddenly motivated its owner to have a long drink, a very long drink. Mrs. Bulton's voice now added to the attack, but she never let go of her end of the yardstick, knowing, I think, that she could appear to have some control as long as she hung on to that stick and hurled screams at this overgrown kid. When Jack had enough water, or enough of the woman bouncing around at the other end of the yardstick, he threw his end of the stick down towards his side. Before Mrs. Bulton could recover, he was back in his desk making grinning eye-contact with all his admiring fellow pupils who knew it was not safe to show any admiration for Jack in this little one-room school house.

Without newspapers, and before TV had invaded this rural community, Jack was as close to being a hero as these kids would ever have. Mrs. Bulton stormed back up to her desk, her shouting and threatening ter-rifying everyone back to their work. She wildly wrote something in a book that the students were sure would be handed to the school inspector, Mr. Floyd, when he made his frightening, twice-yearly visits to the school.

Mrs. Bulton also had a son. For a year or so he came to school with her. Now Mrs. Bulton could not be accused of having played favorites with her son. Her Dennis clearly suffered the full brunt of her teach-er violence, all, it seemed, without much affect. Den-nis was tough. One day when I was visiting the school, Dennis got the older boys to go on the teeter-totter with him. He would get on one end and would direct a collection of boys heavier in total than he was to get up on the other end. Of course, his lighter weight would ensure his place high up in the air at the end of the long board. Then, on a signal from him, the boys would jump off and Dennis' end would come crashing down like a falling rock. He would hit the ground like a thrown rodeo rider, sometimes lie and groan in agony for a moment, and then ask his con-scripted torturers to do it again. One day—for the sto-ries were that he performed these manly feats quite of-ten—he got his arm under the board when it came

crashing down. Clearly his arm was broken. When
without tears, he went in to show his mother his
crooked, disabled arm, he got no sympathy.

The older kids said that at a birthday party at his
house some weeks later, Dennis jumped off the second story roof of his house. He landed wrongly, and
rolling over in the grass in his crash, pushed a tooth
through the skin above his top lip. He went inside to
show his mother. She summarily pushed the tooth
back through the gash above his lip, told him not to
be so silly, and he came back out to play.

Mrs. Bulton wasn't a teacher at the school anymore
by the time I got there. I think I might have been too
terrified of her to learn anything.

I'm sure there's a story that explains why Mrs. Bulton
ruled her world the way she did, and why she was so
unmoved by her son's injuries. Why she was so exer-
cised by a boy drinking water out of a water pail yet
registered no emotion at a son's broken arm or a tooth
sticking out where it was not supposed to be, is a mystery. Some things moved her powerfully and other
events left her unmoved. Something had drained Mrs.
Bulton's compassion away. Somehow the compassion
quotient that God injects into his image-bearers at
their creation got jaded, and it seems Mrs. Bulton was
fighting back. Fighting back was probably her way of
responding to some injustice or injustices visited upon
her. She wanted back what she had lost. Now she was
so angry she just lashed out, or just couldn't and
didn't care anymore. But I don't think Mrs. Bulton
just wanted back what she had lost; I think she wanted
back what had taken her compassion away as well, so
that she could have it all again. If she could have re-

captured what was lost, or dealt with what was taken away from her, she would probably have become a kind, compassionate woman, no longer a victim. A person more like God, who is compassionate and sympathetic every day.

Little Lennie

N ow it's not true that Little Lennie lived in the backwoods, although running water and electricity came to his family home later than it did to much of the rest of Canada. And while he can't remember not having electric lights, he can remember there not being any taps in their house, a pail under the sink to catch the water they dumped, and melting snow in big pails on the stove in winter to provide water to wash the clothes and bathe in. He also remembers a square zinc tub that his mom hung sheets around for some privacy for anyone having a bath in the kitchen. The tub was so small a grown-up could sit in it only if he bent his knees over the edge of the tub and rested his feet outside it on the floor. The only person Little Lennie ever saw do this was his big brother. The bathroom was a biffy 50 yards from the house in the snow, in the frozen seat-board winter and in the paralyzing dark of night. The cold and dark often made the trip to the biffy wholly unnecessary.

Every other summer or so, Little Lennie's family loaded up and traveled to the west coast with whatever used car was still running with the help of his dad's genius. "Jake can make anything mechanical keep running with a bit of bailer wire and a plier," the neighbors used to say. Once he even added some real cranking zip to a slow-starting Ford with an extra battery he built in with its own plywood battery case snuggled down under the hood and electrically paralleled to the one already there. When finally at the coast and at an uncle's garage, those cars that Jake magically kept going got some real work done on them, even if the work was made necessary to avoid having to visit too many relatives. The car was always ship-shape if the family wanted to go to Cultus Lake or up to Mt. Baker "across the line."

Little Lennie remembers the year that "It Was An Itsy Bitsy Yellow Polka-Dot Bikini" was number one on the hit parade, and his teenage siblings and their cousins petitioned their elders to go to the beach park for supper every evening of the holiday. Their hope, of course, was that the adults would get lost in conversation and storytelling, allowing the young people to catch the action on the beach. Teenagers from miles around gathered by the hundreds on the huge docks at Cultus Lake every evening. Someone ingeniously found a way to broadcast the radio hits—the biggest song of the summer, that risqué bikini song, among them—across the waters at a level that everyone in the resort town could easily hear. To teenagers from a less progressive part of the world, this beach, its loud music and the attire it spawned was an unmatched cultural experience.

Little Lennie was too young to notice or care. He had found a building, a bathroom, 100 yards or so back from the beach in the trees that, amazingly, had no less than six flush toilets. Flush toilets. He was mesmerized. If he watched outside carefully enough, he could go into that bathroom when no one else was in there and get a good look at these things. He could flush the toilets and watch the water crashing and cascading around without anyone thinking he was weird and kicking him out. He'd remembered someone back on the farm saying these flush toilets would never catch on. They wasted too much water.

This evening, however, he went from cubicle to cubicle wasting water in all his little boyness. The teenagers could have all the fun they wanted with their dumb songs and their giggling and throwing each other off the dock; this was incredible. He came to the last cubicle. The bowl was almost full; the others had been mostly empty when he tipped their little handles. He pushed down the handle like he had the others and waited to see the water start its counter clockwise journey into the bowels of the earth. But something must be wrong. The water just came up and up and up. Little Lennie stepped back. Water ran over the edge of the white porcelain bowl and down over the side like a spring waterfall. It ran onto the floor and started toward him. He backed away. It just kept coming. He bolted for the swinging brown door and headed across to his parents and the other adults sitting around the remains of their supper picnic, talking and laughing. Little Lennie hunched down beside his dad on the green wool blanket that sometimes covered the front seat of the car and stayed there for the rest of the evening. The whole evening. Even during the three times his dad tried to get the older kids off the dock and away from that awful music, Little Lennie stayed on the blanket. He was terrified; he had done something dastardly back in that big bathroom. Water was spilling everywhere because of him. He shuddered.

A few days later, the family left the coast for their

trip back to the prairies. Lennie sat on the green, plaid seat cover of the front seat safely between his mom and dad and imagined that the water in that great bathroom back at Cultus Lake was still gushing across the floor, and had probably reached the beach by this time. The park authorities with their green uniforms would certainly be looking for who it was that had done this.

The family got home two days later without incident. A couple of weeks later a police car drove up the lane of Little Lennie's family farm. His dad went over to greet the policeman. Little Lennie scooted off the little dirt pile where he played with his toy trucks and tractors and went and hid in the barn.

C hildren live with fear. Adults would laugh at their children's fears, if they could explain them. But fear terrifies, it robs sleep, it causes nightmares, bedwetting and acting out. We forget childhood fears, we adults, and in the main forget the richness of childhood with all its sharpness of feelings and emotions. Yet the things we fear as adults are probably just as silly to God as we would think a kid silly for being paralyzed because he made a toilet run over.

Fear can also be a gift. It's a God-given protective mechanism that keeps us from doing things that probably aren't safe or good for us to do. What fear as a gift means, though, is that fear should inform us, not control us. "The beginning of wisdom is the fear of the Lord," is a biblical statement I grew up with. To fear God is to have awe for God, to let his being inform our life. We are to be controlled by another awareness, the awareness that God is love and mercy and kindness. That knowledge is what can mark the living

of our days, and can allow us to walk lightly, smile easily and die happily when our days are over. Fear is
something we can give to God every day. Once that
fear is properly placed we can live unfettered, unclut-
tered and well.

Tante Helena

ante Helena is not a well woman. Cancer has been ravaging her for years. Her pelvic and hip bones have been eaten through. Two of the vertebrae in her back and her neck need artificial support. Her left arm has been immobilized by a recent break and on her last visit to the specialist, the doctor said Tante Helena's liver is swollen with cancer now, too. So Helena sits most of her days in a large chair, carefully holding her head to one side. "My right arm is still healthy and I can still kiss and love," she smiles.

And it's a good thing she can, for snuggled on that right arm is tiny Nad, a preemie baby born to a fourteen-year-old girl and her fifteen-year-old brother in a culture that has no tolerance for things like this. Poor tiny Nad, not only born wrongly and too soon, but also born with multiple disabilities, was left to die in the hospital. But a social worker intervened and got little Nad to another hospital. The people there, too, said heroic efforts should not be made; the little boy would die.

That was when *Tante* Helena and her husband

heard about tiny Nad, and asked if they could look after him. Since then, Nad has lived on Helena's good
arm, for the first week or so being fed through a tube,
but now taking a tiny bottle. He's growing. *Tante* Helena holds him day and night on her right arm and
talks to him easily because that's the way her head is
bent now, and she kisses him all the time. Baby Nad
is doing all right; so is *Tante* Helena.

As long as we can draw breath, there is something
of value that we can do. *Tante* Helena utilized her
few remaining resources to serve another human even
more helpless. One of the minor Jewish holidays in-
structs the pious poor to go out and find someone
poorer and give them food. We dare not think, ever,
that we are the most needy. Someone else is in greater
need; now is not the time for self-pity. Every day, no
matter what, somebody needs you and me. Who
knows that beggar you gave a meal to on Monday, that
shiverer you handed your coat to on Tuesday, that
shut-in you called on Wednesday, that child you
helped on Thursday, that clerk you said "Thank you!"
to on Friday, that neighbor you assisted on Saturday,
and that usher you appreciated on Sunday, may well
be Jesus. Those you touch are to be treated no differently than you would Jesus.

Touching others is real living, every day. That's seeing God every day, that's letting him flow through you
every day. That's the essence of life. The Good Life.
Living with an everyday God, every day.

About the Author

A perceptive storyteller, Dan thinks deeply about everyday occurrences and draws spiritual reflections from them, inviting his listeners and readers to do the same. As a pastor, Dan uses the medium of storytelling to convey God's message to his congregation both inside and outside the confines of the church walls.

Dan has pastored various churches for the last fifteen years. Prior to that he spent six years as a high school teacher. Dan has a Bachelor of Arts in Sociology from the University of Winnipeg and a Masters of Arts in Jewish Studies and Christian Roots from Jerusalem University College.

In this, his second book, he invites you, the reader, to journey with him on the highways of Europe and the Middle East, through the joys and sorrows of family and ministry encounters and the daily nuances of life that add color and perspective to all we do. In the process, he encourages you to reflect on the many ways God can use the rogues, rascals and rare gems you meet to enrich your life.

Dan is senior pastor at Fraserview Mennonite Brethren Church in Richmond BC. He and his wife Lois have three children: Shoshana, Aila and Levi.